QIGONG OF THE ESSENCE OF TA

THE TEACHINGS OF GRANDMASTER CAI SONG FANG

Warriors Of Stillness

Meditative Traditions
In The Chinese Martial Arts

Volume I

Qigong Of The Center, Essence Of Taijiquan

Teachings of Grandmaster Cai Song Fang

by

Jan Diepersloot

Warriors Of Stillness
Meditative Traditions In The Chinese Martial Arts
Volume I
Qigong Of The Center, Essence Of Taijiquan
Teachings of Grandmaster Cai Song Fang

Jan Diepersloot
Center For Healing & The Arts
POB 369
Walnut Creek, CA 94597

E-mail may be addressed to: jandiep@earthlink.net

Library of Congress Catalog Card Number: 95-96121

ISBN number: 0-9649976-0-6

Book design and graphics by the author.

Dedication

This work is dedicated to the growing community of people who are seeking to develop their practice of the internal martial arts as part of their spiritual path. Namaste.

Acknowledgements

This book would not have become a reality without the help of a large number of people.

First and foremost, of course, I wish to express my deepest gratitude to grandmaster Cai for the kind and systematic sharing of his knowledge.

I am most grateful to master Fong Ha of Berkeley, CA for creating the climate that has attracted, over the last twenty years, such large numbers of gifted teachers and committed students and encouraged them in the joint pursuit of the meditative martial arts.

I wish to thank Marney Ackerman, Rebecca Spalten, Nancy Kieffer and Bruce Wolf for their invaluable editorial assistance. Also Jim Williams for the transliteration of Chinese names.

Lastly, I want to thank the collective membership of Master Cai's classes and workshops, master Fong Ha's Saturday Berkeley Group, and my own students. The overlapping membership of these groups provided the social matrix or context that helped shape and define this book by giving me a constant flow of positive feedback and critical analysis based on intensive and extensive experimentation.

With apologies to all those unintentionally omitted, I thank all the people in the list below for being, or having been, a part of my internal arts life. How blessed we are to be able to share these magnificent practices.

Marney	Ackerman	Henry	Look
Gerhard	Ackermann	Lara	Magruder
Wiltrud	Ackermann	Peter	Marks
Valerie	Adase	Michael	Mayer
Danielle	Almendros	Barbara	McNair
Barbara	Andeno	Jeff	Michel
Renee	Beck	John	Morris
Bill	Brennan	Tim	Muscovitch
Paul	Bruno	Connie	Neary
jane	Chin	Patrick	O'Kiersey
Jane	Church	Eric	Olsen
Margaret	Cullison	Eric	Otto
Peter	Davis	Sue	Otto
MaryBeth	Deans	Barbara	Raif
Gayle	Den Daas	Tim	Racer
Jim	Doxsee	Pam	Rehl
Sara	Dunham	Richard	Rehl
Ofer	Erez	Terry	Rockwell
Amy	Erez	Sandy	Rosenberg
Jack	Fallin	Harold	Rossman
Dan	Farber	Francesca	Roveda
Dave	Fitzgerald	Paul	Samberg
Earl	Flage	Marc	Schuler
Lucy	Flynn	Beverly	Schroeder
George	Fong	Celeste	Sheifer
Vivian	Fong	Sally	Shimuzu
Jim	Gomez	Franklin	Sills
Juan	Gonzales	Elaine	Starkman
Micheline	Ha	Sara	Strange
David	Jamieson	Sifu Paul	Tam
Alberta	Jannusch	Simon	Tam
Robert	Johnson	Brook	Tankle
Jasmine-Rose	Kam	Ming Lee	Tim
Nancy	Kieffer	Margaret	Torn
Glen	Kohler	Tsing Hwa	Tsang
Susan	Hobbs	Mitch	Tsao
Jo	Hurst	Louise	Wang
John	LeBourgeois	Debbie	Wheeler
Bob	Lee	Jim	Williams
Chuck	Lee	Bruce	Wolfe
Higgie	Lerner	Edie	Yap
Rolla	Lewis	Harold	Yap
Mark	Lipman		

CONTENTS

CONTENTS

Author's Introduction: Warriors of Stillness

PART 1
BEING MINDFUL OF THE CENTER
HOW TO CULTIVATE RELAXATION AND INTEGRATION FOR HEALTH

PART II
BEING MINDFUL OF
THE FOUNDATION & SPHERE
HOW TO CULTIVATE RELAXATION AND INTEGRATION FOR MARTIAL ARTS

PART III
BEING MINDFUL OF THE CONNECTION
HOW TO USE RELAXATION AND INTEGRATION FOR MARTIAL ARTS

WARRIORS OF STILLNESS

Warriors Of Stillness

The Chinese martial arts are a vast and fascinating body of principles and techniques, theories and practices, that developed over time in an attempt to gain control over physical human conflict. One very interesting feature of the Chinese martial arts is the differentiation into the external and internal martial arts. In general the external schools are far more numerous. Based on the obvious uses of the energy of (external) movement and physical strength, they present a common sense method of self-defense training. The internal martial arts are far fewer in number, there being only three main schools: *taijiquan (t'ai chi ch'uan), xingyiquan (hsing i ch'uan)* and *baguazhang (pa kua chang)*. The training methods seem more mysterious because internal martial artists move very slowly or not at all. Because they are are subtler and deeper, they are less accessible to the majority of people, who simply don't have the time or desire for deep and prolonged study.

One very interesting feature of the Chinese martial arts is their differentiation into the external and internal martial arts.

Within the schools of the internal family, there is a further polarization. The majority of internal family teachers and practitioners, like their counterparts in the external schools, still emphasize the practice of forms, the choreographed sequences of movements, as the path to mastery. They rely on the practice of stillness and postural meditation only as an adjunct or complementary practice. On the other hand, the minority current within the internal schools deemphasize the practice of movement and forms and in some cases reject them altogether in favor of the exclusive practice of stillness in postural meditation as the path to mastery.

i

What makes the internal or meditative martial arts both internal and meditative is precisely the use of stillness as opposed to movement. Stillness is the ultimate weapon to be used against the adversary. In summary, it can be said that the external martial arts are based on the energy of movement, whereas the internal martial arts are based on the movement of energy. The external arts are based on strength and movement, the internal on awareness and stillness. The external are based on the principle that the "best defense is offense" while the internal on the principle that "the best offense is defense".

The "Warriors of Stillness" is a trilogy which investigates the relationship between the Chinese meditative and martial arts. A volume will be devoted to the meditative current within each of the three martial arts that constitute the *neijiaquan (nei chia ch'uan)* or the "internal family" group: *taijiquan, xingyiquan* and *baguazhang*.

The external martial arts are based on the energy of movement, whereas the internal martial arts are based on the movement of energy.

This first volume, entitled *Wuji Qigong and the Essence of Taijiquan* explores the relationship between the meditative and martial arts within the *taijiquan* system as practiced by Grandmaster Cai Songfang from Shanghai and Canton. The second volume is tentatively entitled *The Method of Awareness in the Martial Arts*. In it I will present a detailed account of the creation of *yiquan (i ch'uan)* and its subsequent transmission, including my experiences with Masters Fong Ha (Xia Changfang, Hia Ch'ang Fang,), Han Xingyuan (Han Hsing Yuan) and Yu Pengxi (Yu P'eng Hsi). Volume three of the trilogy will present the meditative tradition within the *baguazhuang* system. Accompanying each respective volume will be a CD and a docu-

Introduction by the Author

I was impressed with the quality of Master Ha's lineage, the quality of his movements and his desire to seek out the essence of things.

Master Fong Ha

mentary/instructional videotape for a complete package of self-learning.

ooo

In the early seventies, I followed up on a long-standing interest in the martial arts by enrolling in a college karate course. However, I soon became disenchanted with the authoritarian climate, the hard and violent training methods and I dropped out. Then, in January 1975, a friend draggged me along to a *taijiquan* class taught by Master

Yang Style Taijiquan -Lines of Transmission

Introduction by the Author

Fong Ha in Berkeley. I left the class impressed with the quality of his movement as well as the superiority of his lineage. As a teenager, Master Ha studied with Dong Yingjie, a famous Yang stylist, and later he became a student of Yang Shouzhong, the fourth generation banner carrier of Yang family style of *taijiquan* .

Besides that, there were a couple of other reasons I signed on with Master Ha. Not only was he personable and open, but he also seemed to be the kind of person who was interested in searching out the essence of things without getting sidetracked by appearances. In my almost twenty years of uninterrupted association with him, these initial intuitions have been borne out over and over again.

It took me about six months or so to learn the form, the sequence of 108 linked postures orginally created by Yang Chengfu. I was in heaven, knowing that I had really found "my thing." Most of all, I loved the nature of the movement itself, at once loosening and strenthening the body as well as helping to quiet the always too busy mind.

The practice resolved certain deep seated needs and issues for me relating back to childhood. As a kid, I had been a "natural" athlete, although a very frustrated one. Due to the family situation, I had not been able to develop my athletic abilities. Finding *taijiquan* at age 35 was a god-send. I quickly realized that I had stumbled onto something really precious. I had found a sport and discipline in which age does not matter, where the question of being "over the hill" physically is irrelevant, where I can continue to grow and improve until the day I die.

> **I had found a sport and discipline in which age does not matter, where the question of being over the hill physically is irrelevant, where you can continue to grow and improve until the day you die.**

My own interest in the internal or meditative dimension of the martial arts developed with reluctance. When I started *taiji* with Master Ha , I was totally enchanted by the graceful movement of the form. I believed that in this type of movement, without having to be still, I could reap the same benefits that many of my friends who had begun practicing sitting meditation were reporting. In other words, I thought I could have my cake and eat it, too. Indeed, in typical Western ignorance, my initial conception was that the peaceful, meditating monk and the fighting warrior were mutually exclusive. One was boring; one was exciting. It took some time for me to begin to understand they shared a deep reciprocity: The martial artist must seek to cultivate the peace of the monk as much as the monk must seek to cultivate the fearless attitude of a warrior.

The martial artist must seek to cultivate the peace of the monk, as much as the monk must seek to cultivate the fearless attitude of the warrior.

Six months after I started studying *taiji* movement, Master Ha returned from a trip to China reporting he had found a great *gongfu (kung fu)* master whose main practice was standing meditation, just being still. Master Ha announced that that would be the direction of his own development and *taijiquan* practice. From my limited perspective, I was not pleased with this new direction, to say the least. I thought seriously of finding another teacher who would not require getting into this silly standing meditation stuff. I talked to Master Ha about it, and he said "Oh, why don't you just try it for a hundred hours to see what it feels like. A hundred hours is not much, really. At forty minutes a day, it will take you five months to do a hundred hours." I agreed that was not an unreasonable thing to ask for in a serious tryout. After a couple of months of battling initial reluctances, frustration, and feelings of "I just can't wait till this forty minutes is over," I started looking forward to the sessions. Something mysterious and significant was happening to me. An alchemical process had been started and even though I was unable to articulate it, I was certainly able to feel it.

What changed a budding interest on my part to an obsession of sorts was meeting Han Xingyuan, the Master who so excited Master Ha. In 1976 and 1977, Fong brought Han Xingyuan for visits of several months duration. During this time I had the opportunity to work and study with Han Xingyuan on a daily basis. Master Han was a formidable man with unparalled martial ability. He had been trained in the *xingyiquan* and *yiquan* systems by the originator of the latter, the great Wang Xiangzhai himself.

The practice with Master Han was an intense ordeal, a baptism by fire. Basic practice consisted of holding a minimum of eight postures for a minimum of five minutes each-- a total of 40 minutes standing meditation. This was

Yiquan Masters

Wang Xianzhai, founder
1886-1963

Han Xingyuan

Dr. Yu Pengshi

followed by another hour of moving exercise patterns and walking meditation patterns. The basic practice was to keep the body in correct alignment and posture with the continuous appplication of the conscious mind, or intention. Under the stern tutelage of Master Han, the strenuous work began to reshape my body and its connection to my mind. The first inklings of the meaning of integration began to stir in my awareness. The categories of center, centerline, foundation and sphere became more and more physical, experiential realities rather than abstract ideas. I began to get glimpses of how the proper integration of the center, centerline, foundation and sphere would result in the very special ability of discharging the bodys "integral force."

As an investigator I realized that the investigation would entail duplicating the results in myself. Only then could I legitimately write about the answer to the question of how such extraordinary fighting skills can be developed in total stillness.

This first introduction to the economy of Mind and Movement by Master Han of the *yiquan* sytem was soon reinforced by a second authority. In 1981, another *yiquan* master and top student of Wang Xiangzhai, Dr.Yu Pengxi settled in the Bay Area Once again, Fong was his main interpreter, and so I also studied *yiquan* with Yu Pengxi for several years, profiting from his own specialized techniques of awareness (sensitivity/intention) and strength (integration) training.

Here the mystery hit me with full force: the Masters Han and Yu developed their extrordinary martial arts skills solely as the result of standing meditation, in short just by being still. As a researcher and journalist, there was a story in this apparent paradox that was worth pursuing. As an investigator I realized that the investigation would entail duplicating the results in myself. Only then could I legitimately answer the question of how such extraordi-

Introduction by the Author

nary fighting skills can be developed in total stillness. At the point of this writing, I have been doing standing meditation for almost 20 years and I believe I have, through the experience of my practice, achieved the understanding necessary to present both the theory and practice involved in using stillness as a defensive tool and offensive weapon.

ooo

During the seventies, it was Master Ha's habit to return every year to Hong Kong and study with his teachers Yang Shouzhong and Han Xingyuan. There, along with his friends, he broadened his horizons by searching for and meeting many great martial artists of various schools.

A turning point came in 1979 when mainland China opened up its borders. At the urging of one of his friends in Hong Kong, Master Ha agreed to hand deliver a gift to Master Cai Songfang while Fong was visiting Canton. Master Cai was reputed to be a *taiji* grandmaster who had popularized *wuji (wu chi)* meditation in the local hospitals as recuperative therapy, and also established a reputation as "the king of push-hands" in Canton. In recognition of his achievements, Master Cai was chosen in 1987 as the representative of Guangdong province to the National Committe on *qigong (ch'i kung)* research. Masters Ha and Cai immediately developed a strong and lasting rapport. Fortunately for his students, Master Ha always took his video camera along on his journeys and did ample taping. Thus from the very beginning, we all became quite familiar with the nature of Master Cai's work and practice. Finally, in 1987, Master Cai was able to come to the U.S.

Grandmaster Cai was the representative of Guangdong province to the National Committee of Qigong research

What was so amazing and appealing to us about Master Cai was the similarity of his practice compared with the *yiquan* system, i.e. standing meditation. Here we had tapped into a similar current in the *taijiquan* system as had led to the creation of the *yiquan* system out of the *xingyiquan* system. Likewise, in the *taijiquan* tradition, underneath the proliferation of family styles and their innumerable forms, there runs a deep current that finds the source of all movement in the stillness of postural meditation. That is, Master Cai, like the *yiquan* system, puts primary emphasis on the development of the *yi (i)*, or mind intent. Additionally, like the *yiquan* system, Master Cai's main practice is standing meditation. Like the *yiquan* practitioners, Master Cai does not practice forms. In fact, though in the Yang style lineage, he does not practice the long form or any set sequences. The longest sequence of movement Master Cai ever does is "Grasping the Bird's Tail", consisting of ward-off, rollback, press and push.

In the Chinese worldview and philosophy, *taiji* comes from *wuji* : all being and movement comes from, and must ultimately return to the stillness and emptiness of the void.

Within the *taijiquan* tradition, the practice of *wuji* standing meditation has long been an open secret. Theoretically, it has been there all along for anyone to treasure, except that only very few were initiated into its actual practice Read any book on *taiji* and somewhere, usually in the very beginning, it will explain that in the Chinese worldview and philosophy, *taiji* comes from *wuji* : all being and movement comes from, and must ultimately return to the stillness and emptiness of the void. The implications of this truth are profound and staggering. Yet not one of the books I have read on *taiji* devotes more than a paragraph or so to the *wuji* posture and its uses, while exhaustively detailing all the other postures and the movements linking them.

Introduction by the Author

Yang Cheng Fu, the founder of Yang style *taijiquan*, kept the *wuji* standing meditation practice a zealously guarded secrets of the Yang family. Only on rare occasions did Yang Cheng Fu share his secret practice of *wuji* standing meditation with outsiders. One of the lucky recipients of this knowledge was Mr. Ye Dami, who received it from Yang Chengfu in the late 1920s when he was teaching in Shanghai. Mr. Ye Dami in turn transmitted the knowledge to Master Cai Songfang during the 1950s.

Wuji qigong is, first and foremost, the cultivation of energy skills in the stillness of the center.

After trying for several years, Master Ha was finally able to arrange for Master Cai to come for a six month visit to the U.S. As we gathered in the park across from Fong's house on a sunny cold winter morning in early January 1987, the mood of our *taijiquan* group was vibrant with expectation. Master Ha had picked up Master Cai at the airport the night before. Finally, we were about to meet him in person. Then the door of Fong's house opened, and they emerged. My first impressions were of a big man, maybe 5-9, 190-200 lbs, somewhat pear shaped with a bit of a pot belly. He didn't look very intimidating at all. Very animated, he talked and gestured with gusto. As they approached, I noticed his suit was still creased from being folded and packed in the suitcase. His outgoing, ready smile and somewhat shy enthusiasm were immediately infectious.

After a minimum of formalities, Master Ha came right to the point. "O.K. Jan, try him." What he was saying to me was to "play" push-hands with Master Cai. Push-hands is a *taiji* practice and game which cultivates and tests one's

Master Cai

sensitivity, equilibrium, and a special type of strength called "integral force," or *pieng jing.* Master Cai was not only humble, he was humbling. I tried my repertoire of tricks and strategies to no avail. Every time I pushed or touched him, I was thrown back 6, 8, or 10 feet. What was weird and fascinating was that Master Cai did not even move as he threw me away like a bouncing ball. He discharged his energy from a completely still position. And no matter where on the body I touched him, my energy was first absorbed and neutralized, and then repulsed and thrown back. And not only back, but also sideways, up and down, wherever he wanted. He was in complete control. Even when we were not touching, I knew I was powerless. I knew that he already had my center. I also knew that I had no idea where his center was.

And no matter where on the body I touched him, my energy was first absorbed and neutralized, and then repulsed and thrown back. And not only back, but also sideways, up and down.

I had been practicing and playing *taiji* and related arts for almost a dozen years. Playing push-hands over the years with many, many people had made me feel that I had developed something. "Pushing" with Master Cai made me realize just how incredibly small that achievement was. My first lesson with Master Cai was a well deserved and welcome lesson in humility. At the same time, Master Cai opened a vista of incredible growth possibilities and levels of possible achievement I had never dreamed existed in the art. I think my experience is shared by numerous martial artists of different disciplines who have sought out Master Cai. Master Cai's reputation as one of the premier contemporary Chinese martial and healing artist, is continually growing in China and around the world.

Again, what really makes Master Cai's achievement so remarkable is the fact that his main practice consists of standing meditation only. As mentioned, he calls this method *wuji qigong (wu chi ch'i kung)*. *Wuji* means the "ultimate void." It is that place in us where it is as still as the void that contains us. *Qigong* is the art or skill of cultivating energy. *Wuji qigong* is first and foremost the cultivation of energy skills in the stillness of the center. Master Cai's unique achievement in the martial arts is his mastery of the paradox that the perfection of stillness leads to the control of movement. In his work as a martial artist, Master Cai is pushing the art of "achieving more by doing less" toward its ultimate limit of "achieving all by doing nothing."

The common essence of the meditative and martial arts is the attempt to transcend the limitations imposed on us by biology.

As with Masters Han and Yu, encountering Master Cai once again challenged the seeker and investigator in me with the question, "How is this possible and what are the implications?" To me the story of Master Cai and his art is interesting for more than his individual accomplishment. It has deep implications for the training of both body and mind that could revolutionize both health maintenance practices and optimize performance achievement in any sport or discipline. In a nutshell, the relevance of Master Cai's work to the modern human dilemma is this: The common essence of the meditative and martial arts is the attempt to transcend the limitations of biology, allowing us to consciously confront and deal with situations of stress and danger .

As human beings, we have two distinctly different neuro-hormonal systems. One is designed to deal with

Introduction by the Author

Master Cai playing with the author

Every time I pushed or touched him, I was thrown back 6, 8, or 10 feet. What was weird and fascinating was that Master Cai did not even move as he threw me away like a bouncing ball.

emergencies such as fight or flight and involves the sympathetic nervous system and the pituitary-adrenal hormonal cicuits. The other is designed to deal with the more pleasurable rhythms of daily life and involves primarily the para-sympathetic nervous system. These neurohormonal systems can be referred to, respectively, as the neurophysiology of emergency and the neurophysiology of harmony. The accomplishment of the training in the meditative and martial arts is precisely the ability to transcend and suppress the functioning of the sympathtic, pituitary-adrenal system and continue to operate with calm equanimity in the face of extreme danger, including, ultimately, the encounter with death itself.

The dilemma of post-industrial civilization is the widespread (psychological) internalization and the (social) institutionalization of the neurophysiology of emergency. We have literally incorporated the fight-flight syndrome in our bodies and minds, perpetuating our adrenalin addiction. We have been culturally conditioned to need and crave the intense stimuli of anxiety, fear and terror, anger and rage ; we are junkies driven on by our ceaselessly operating sympathetic nervous system. Unbalanced because deprived of sufficient parasympathetic stimulation, pleasure and relaxation, we are sorely lacking in the necessary tools to deal with the endemic social stress we have embodied in our systems. The quest of the next century, indeed the quest of the next millennium, will be to learn how to cultivate our own individual neurophysiology of harmony. Because we need the ability to transcend the neurophysiology of emergency which has us in its grip, we must acquire the skills and knowledge of meditators and martial artists such as Master Cai.

Everyday life in our hyper-competitive, commercial culture of "modern civilization" has come to resemble a jungle or battlefield. It recreates the internalization of the psychophysiology of emergency both in people's psychophysiological make-up and the social structures which mediate their interactions. The continuing battle for survival has created a dysfunctional populace in which the relationship of people to themselves is warped to the extent that the dysfunctional has become the norm. For the norm in this civilization is for people to have no relationship to their center and root. They are so filled with

Increasing numbers of people are turning to the *wuji-taiji* method of awareness as their therapeutic tool of choice to help them deal with the oppressive reality of our stress inducing culture.

xvi

stress and anxiety that they are incapable of perceptivity and empathy in their interactions with others.

Increasing numbers of people are turning to the *wuji-taiji* method of awareness as their therapeutic tool of choice to help them deal with the oppressive reality of our stress-inducing culture. Out of this, the unfortunate situation has arisen where people are searching but not finding or receiving the real benefits. At present, very few therapists have sufficiently mastered the *wuji-taiji* method of awareness to be able to appreciate the depths and range of its tranformative power, let alone being qualified to use it in their therapeutic work with clients. And there are also very few *taiji* teachers who have the therapeutic insight, ability and credentials to investigate and develop the therapeutic dimension of the *wuji-taiji* method of awareness.

As a therapy of formidable tranformative powers, the *wuji taiji* method of awareness is a self reinforcing and self correcting experiential feedback loop between the categories of Being, Movement, and Interaction.

Although not a therapist, I have experienced the profound therapeutic benefits of the *wuji-taiji* method of awareness first hand. Thus, as a martial art teacher, I approach the teaching of this art with the heart of a therapist. With the writing of this book, apart from its value as pure research, I hope to stimulate more therapists to take up the practice of *wuji-taiji* method of awareness and incorporate it in their practice. I also want to stimulate the teachers the *wuji-taiji* system to become more therapeutically oriented in their teaching methods and relationship with their students.

As a therapy of formidable tranformative powers, the *wuji -taiji* method of awareness is a way of life, a strategy,

Early morning standing meditation practice with Master Cai

and a practice. It is a self-reinforcing and self-correcting experiential feedback loop among the categories of Being, Movement, and Interaction. First, you practice stillness in order to discover the structure of your Being. Then you learn how to Move this Being, and third, this Being learns how to Interact with other Beings. Interactive practices with other Beings proceed from the physical in push-hands to the non-physical and more subtle field interactions. Awareness of field interactions leads back to the practice of stillness as *the* method for increasing

Introduction by the Author

awareness of our own Being and those of others. While this is roughly the logical sequence of events, in actual life and daily practice, I experience Being, Moving and Interaction as skills that are continually and mutually honing each other.

In my experience, the *wuji-taiji* method of awareness begins to turn the dysfunctional into the functional, the normal into the natural, by teaching us how to find our Center and cultivate strength there. Working with relaxation and integration, gradually helped me manage my stress and anxiety and alleviate my migraines. Over time I learned to exert a measure of control over the autonomic nervous system and reverse the psychophysiology of emergency to the psychophysiology of harmony as the dominant mode of my behavior and being. By enabling people to discover and draw psycho-physical strength from their center, the *wuji-taiji* method of awareness slowly instills in its practitioners a new way of being with and in themselves, a way of inner peace and security predisposing them to deal with equanimity and empathy in their social relations.

Through awareness of the structure of my being, that is, the interrelationship between my centerpoint, centerline, root foundation and sphere of extension, I learned new and natural parameters of movement. I gained insight into the grammar, or rules according to which we must move the center point, centerline, foundation and sphere in order to optimize both stability and agility. Through the practice of mindfulness in Being and Movement, gradually the great awareness dawned on me: To the degree that we learn to operate from our physical center, we stabilize our mental-emotional center and increase our experiences of joy and ecstasy.

Pushhands therapy teaches us how to win in a conflict situation by relaxing under pressure, yielding to invasive forces in order to bend and redirect them back at the opponent, rather than bruting it out, stiffening up and trying to resist with force.

To my mind what makes the *wuji-taiji* method of awareness so special as therapy is that it goes beyond teaching us how to find the source of our strength inwardly, in our center. The partnered exercises of *taiji* push-hands further hone and test our new found confidence in our center by meeting challenges to our center from our opponent/partner. Push-hands therapy teaches us how to win in a conflict situation by relaxing under pressure, yielding to invasive forces in order to bend and redirect them back at the opponent, rather than bruting it out, stiffening up and trying to resist with force. As we gain skill in push-hands, we learn how to read our opponents better by making our touch lighter and lighter, cultivating and playing with the subtler levels of field awareness. Learning and relearning the lessons of neutralizing and discharging energy, "push-hands play therapy" has taught me, in my interaction with people, how to operate with strength, ease and security from the center of my sphere of

Introduction by the Author

being while touching people lightly with the periphery of my sphere of being. Playing with subtler and subtler energies and awareness, I've learned to expand limitlessly to encompass the interacting fields of all beings that constitute, to use Don Juan's words, the "bubble of my perception" and being. Ultimately I found the therapeutic benefits from pushhand practice and field awareness to be the ability to flow and cope with the world in a more harmonious and productive manner, harming none, being harmed by none and getting things done.

The martial art therapy of the *wuji-taiji* method of awareness has a *yin* and *yang* side to it. Its greatest achievement is the *yin* aspect, the development of awareness and control in the skill of neutralizing and keeping the peace. However, in its *yang* aspect, the *wuji-taiji* method of awareness delivers the power to enforce the peace through the development of the power of deadly integral force that can be discharged with a mere intention. Unique as a therapeutic martial art, the *wuji-taiji* method of awareness gives us access to the expanded perceptual awareness and physical powers (integral force) which the organism can display under conditions of extreme emergency while maintaining the operation of the psycho-physiology of harmony.

Thus, the *wuji-taiji* method of awareness training provides the conditions for the development of the compassionate personality. By transcending the psychophysiology of emergency it teaches us to how to use the power acquired through our practice to interact with/in the world in a responsible and wise manner. Nobody demon-

Unique as a therapeutic martial art, the *wuji-taiji* method of awareness gives us access to the expanded perceptual awareness and physical powers (integral force) which the organism can display under conditions of extreme emergency while maintaining the operation of the psycho-physiology of harmony.

strates better than Master Cai how the *wuji-taiji* method of awareness is one of compassionate interaction. Both in the conduct of his life and in the methods of his teaching , Master Cai epitomizes how knowing one's own center and that of those we come in contact with in push-hands and energy field play can be used to shore people up rather than upsetting them, stabilizing rather than destabilizing them. And this is why, in the final analysis, he has become such an important role model for me, both as a person and as a teacher. He has been able to use and develop his *wuji-taiji* knowledge as a spiritual path method to refine his character, personality and spirit.

Master Cai is a devout Buddhist and follower of Ch'an Master Xuan Hua (Hsuan Hua), the 9th generation patriarch of the Weiyang (Wei-yang) lineage, and the 19th generation patriarch in China beginning with the Bhodidharma. In the teaching of his art, as in his life, Master Cai is a personification of the Buddhist ideals of simplicity and humility, manifesting a complete absence of ego , pretentiousness and ostentation. His teaching art also embodies the Buddhist values of cultivating compassionate temperament and generosity of spirit; he is habitually in a good mood and filled with humorous insight, yet appropriately serious and forthcoming when required. These traits are particularly illustrated in his teaching methods of the martial art uses of *wuji-taiji*. His compassion, for example, is clearly demonstrated in his push-hands practice. No matter what level the development of his opponent, Master Cai operates just a single notch above them and with the sole purpose of teaching. With a minimum of strength and effort exerted, the nature of the

> Master Cai operates just a single notch above them and with the sole purpose of teaching. With a minimum of strength and effort exerted, the nature of the relationship is clearly communicated, and the knowledge of refined control through awareness is passed on continually in living interaction.

Introduction by the Author

relationship is clearly communicated, and the knowledge of refined control through awareness is passed on continually in living interaction. His patience and generosity of character is also immediately and consistently evident. He plays as much with rank beginners as he does with more advanced students, trying to nurture each and every one precisely according to the individual's needs , never hurrying what can't be hurried, or demanding what can't be achieved.

Speaking for all who have had the good fortune to cross paths with Master Cai, I wish to conclude by simply saying "Thank you. From the bottom of our hearts, we thank you."

Berkeley, Class of '91

WUJI QIGONG AND THE ESSENCE OF TAIJIQUAN

A Note on Methodology

After Master Cai's1987 visit, I collected and compiled my thoughts and understandings of Master Cai's teaching in a small booklet entitled *Wuji Qigong and the Essence of Taijiquan : the Teachings of Grandmaster Cai Songfang."* Since Master Cai in his visit had met, played with and impressed many people from different martial arts disciplines and touched the lives of many people, my booklet got quite a wide and favorable reading in the rarefied stratosphere of the internal martial arts world. In the spring of 1990, I had the opportunity to deepen my appreciation of Master Cai's art. Master Ha took me and our friend Sandy Rosenberg along on a trip to Hong Kong and Canton, where we visited and worked with Master Cai almost daily.

One year later, in the spring of 1991, Master Cai once again visited with Master Ha for a six months. My friends were already "bugging" me about another edition of the book, so this time I was better prepared. I attended classes almost daily not only as a student but also as a researcher and journalist, complete with taperecorder. My methodology was simple. Everytime Master Cai would say something insightful, give instructions or offer analyses, I would turn around discreetly and repeat it into the tape recorder. Also, I continually elicited comments from my classmates.

All these materials, quotations and interpretations I faithfully transcribed into my Macintosh , thus steadily building and organizing my database. Being able to readily manipulate the data on the computer has enabled me to allow it to organize itself, to find its own structure and pattern. In writing this book, I have tried to do two things: (1) allow Master Cai to speak for himself, using almost verbatim what he said in English, or translated if he said something in Chinese and (2) report on the experience of my own growth in skill and insight as a result of following his teachings.

Introduction by the Author

A Note On Transliteration

The Transliteration Of Chinese Names and Terms into English is always problematical. In this book I have chosen, in the main, to follow the pinyin method of transliteration. However, the first time any Chinese term or name is spelled, the Wade-Giles system of transliteration is added in parentheses for comparison. If, besides the pinyin and the Wade-Giles there are other known spellings, particularly of proper names, they are also added in the parenthesis. For example, the first mention of *taijiquan* will be *taijiquan (t'ai chi ch'uan, tai chi chuan),* or Grandmaster Cai's full name will the first time be rendered as *Cai Songfang (Ts'ai Sung Fang, Choy Soong Fong).* A complete list of names and terms used in given in Appendix I.

A Note On The Graphics

When I was collecting the research material for this book, I was quite conscientious audiowise, constantly recording Mr. Cai's every utterance. Unfortunately, I was less diligent from the visual point of view, only occasionally bringing my camera. Consequently my visual record of master Cai's stay consisted of a bunch of poor photographs. But, rather than not use them at all, I decided to combine them in montages and/or otherwise subject them to various computer modification techniques in an effort to visually convey the energetic feeling of his ideas and practices.

J.D.

PART 1

BEING MINDFUL OF THE CENTER

HOW TO CULTIVATE AWARENESS OF
RELAXATION AND INTEGRATION FOR HEALTH

Chapter 1

Cultivating The CenterPoint

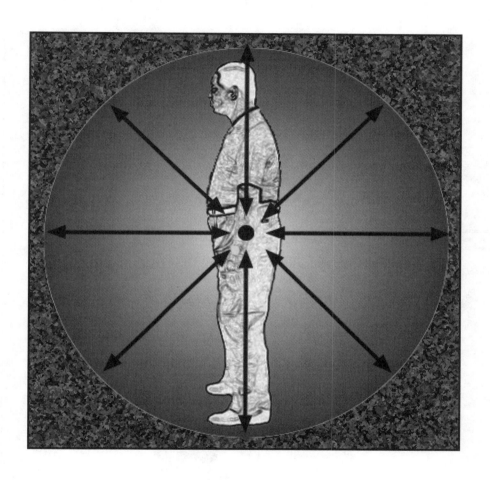

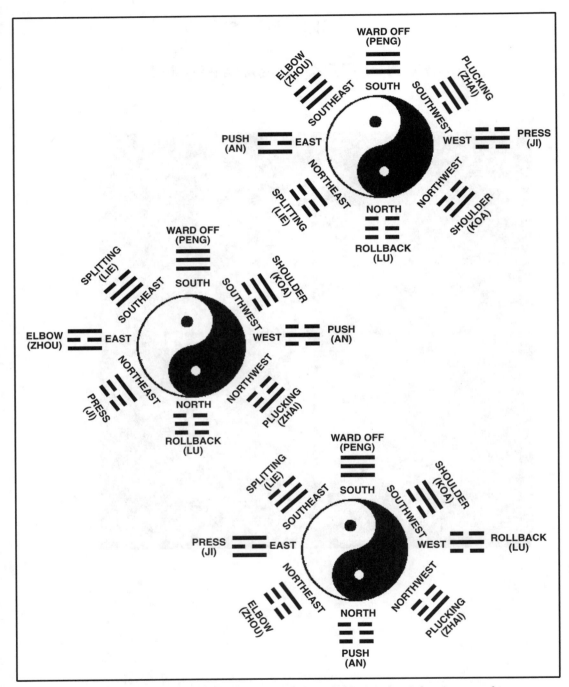

Fig. 1.1 Three different mandalas correlating the eight trigrams of the I Ching with the eight fundamental taiji techniques

Historical And Philosophical Notes

In the olden days, *taijiquan* was often referred to as the art of *shisan shi (shih san shih)*. *Shisan shi* has been variously translated as thirteen postures, methods, or movements. The *shisan shi* was further subdivided into the five attitudes or steps and the eight directions or techniques. The five steps are *zhongding (chung ting)* or central equilibrium, shifting forward, shifting backward, turning left, and turning right. The eight basic techniques consisted of the four main directions and the four corners. The main directions are *peng* or ward-off, *lu* or roll-back, *an* or push, and *ji (chi)* or press. The four corners are *cai (ts'ai)*, or plucking, *lie (lieh)* or wristing, *zhou (chou)* or elbowing, and *kao (k'ao)* or shouldering (leaning).

In his book, *"Advanced Yang Style Tai Chi Chuan,* Yang Jingming (Yang Ching Ming, Yang Jwing-Ming) writes that beginning with Zhang Sanfeng (Chang San Feng), generally regarded as the originator of *taijiquan*, many attempts have been made in the history of Chinese medical and philosophical thought to (1) correlate the five steps with the five element theory of mutual production and destruction and (2) correlate the eight basic directions with the eight trigrams of the *Yijing* (I Ching) and their meanings. However, it seems that the Chinese penchant for looking for meaningful correspondences created a number of opposing systems (three are presented in *fig.1.1*), none of which, concludes Yang Jingming, "are completely reasonable and without discrepancy."

The fundamental *taiji* experience is the movement of the human structure as the movement of a ball or sphere.

In this book we will not concern ourselves with these traditional attempts at making correlations. Instead we will focus solely on the internal structure of the thirteen methods and relate it to the fundamental *taiji* experience in which the movement of the structure of the human being is experienced as the movement of a ball or sphere. This perspective will allow us to understand the five steps as polarity aspects of possible CenterLine movements and the eight directions as basic techniques of using energy by the sphere constituted by our arms. Within, the eight directions, furthermore, we will argue the case the four main directions describe the vertical dimension of the

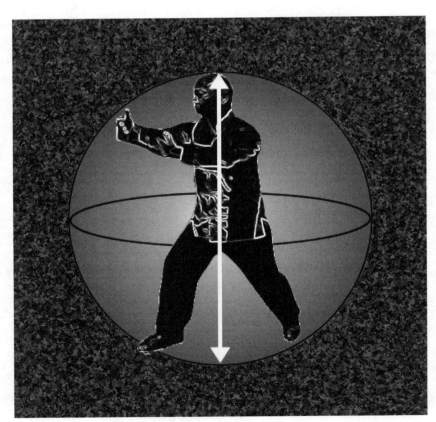

Fig. 1.2 The Vertical and Horzontal Circles of the Human Sphere

taiji sphere, and the four corner directions describe the horizontal aspect of the human sphere *(fig. 1.2)*.

Song of central equilibrium

**We are centered,
stable and still as a mountain
Our *qi* sinks to the *dantian (tan t'ien)*
we are as if suspended from above
Our spirit is concentrated within and
our outward manner perfectly composed
receiving and issuing energy are
both the work of an instant**

The *Song of central equilibrium*, like other *taijiquan* classics, describes central equilibrium as the most essential of the thirteen basic skills of *taijiquan*. This is because it is central equilibrium which gives rise to the *yin-yang* polarity basic to the other twelve methods. Out of *wuji* (the stillnes and non-action of central equilibrium) originates *taiji* or the *yin-yang* of movement and action. Thus without central equilibrium the polarities of empty and solid, or substantial and insubstantial would not exist; therefore the other twelve postures/methods are all subordinate to central equilibrium and can never be dissociated from it. Indeed, strictly speaking, there is no fixed form for any manoever, but all forms or methods are based on central equilibrium. The skill of central equilibrium combines the *yi* (mind) and *qi* (energy) with the eight directions and five steps of the thirteen methods.

In order to do the *taijiquan* movements properly, you must have *zhongding* . But you can have *zhongding* and not know any set of *taijiquan*.

When standing, *zhongding* or central equilibrium stabilizes our center of gravity like a balance scale. In movement, it controls our momentum, and in (martial) action, to paraphrase the classics, it enables the feet to act as the root, enables the legs to propagate the force, enables the waist to direct the force, and enables the fingers to express it. Thus the relationship between *taijiquan* and *zhongding* can be summed up as follows: In order to do the *taijiquan* movements properly, you must have *zhongding* . You can have *zhongding* and not know any set of *taijiquan*. *Taijiquan* movements require central stability, but central stability does not require any particular movements.

Fig. 1.3 Wuji generating Taiji

Closely associated with central equilibrium is the frequently stated principle in the *Tao Te Ching* that "*taiji* comes from *wuji*." *(Fig. 1.3)* This refers to the fact that movement (energy) is a temporal event which begins and ends in stillness. *Ji* means beginning and *wu* is a negation, so that *wuji* means before the beginning, i.e., the big void or nothingness. Perhaps "potential" would be a better term to describe *wuji*. The symbol for *wuji* is the circle with the dot in the middle. The circle represents the infinite emptiness of the void that surrounds our being. The dot represents the emptiness of the void that exists at the very center of our being. The primal *yin-yang* dynamic that governs our movement and energy originates from the *wuji* center. It is expressed in the classical *taiji* symbol of interpenetrating fishes.

When Yang Chengfu created the classical sequence or form, he prominently incorporated this principle. The movement of the *taiji* sequence he created both begins and ends in the stillness of the *wuji* posture. Thus the *wuji* standing meditation Master Cai teaches provides the purest form of central equilibrium training. Stripped of all extraneous motion, only in the stillness of the *wuji* posture can our mind truly cultivate the sensation of *zhongding* or central equilibrium, penetrate into its mysteries and reap its ultimate rewards of insight and ability. In a nutshell, these rewards are:

The *wuji* standing meditation Master Cai teaches provides the purest form of *zhongding* or Central Equilibrium training.

- **as the center of physical gravity, the *wuji* center controls our movement in space.**
- **as the center of biological growth, the *wuji* center controls our unfolding in time.**
- **as the center of integration the *wuji* center is the key to our structural integrity.**
- **as the center of breath, the *wuji* center functions to maintain proper metabolic regulation.**
- **as the center of awareness, the *wuji* center changes the perception of space and time.**

There is an abundance of so-called songs in the classics. Besides the pure esthetics of the poetry, the songs were important educational tools in the transmission of all the arts, including *taijiquan* —short pithy or poetic formulations of vital points easily committed to memory by students.

In that spirit, I have here endeavored to compile a "Song of *Wuji Qigong*", from the instructions I have heard Master Cai give on numerous occasions while teaching and conducting introductory workshops on *Wuji Qigong* meditation.

> **stand with the feet parallel the width of the shoulders**
> **keep the knees unlocked and expanding,**
> **feel as if they're squeezing a big boulder**
> **relaxing the hips and keeping the pelvis tucked**
> **expand the lower back and keep the abdomen sucked**
> **"hollowing the chest and rounding the back"**
> **the arms hang naturally by the side**
> **holding your head high as if suspended from sky**
> **tongue touching palate, close your eyes**
> **sink your awareness down into the belly**
> **naturally breathing in and out**
> **while aligning the three points on a straight line**
> **let the *qi* fill your body**
> **and peace will fill your mind**

The Geography Of The Lower Torso

In the *taijiquan* classics, the advice for correct posture is to "eliminate the hollows and the protuberances." The main "hollow" to be filled here is the small of the back, while the protruberances to be flattened are the abdomen and the buttocks. This is the natural, i.e. structurally optimal posture as opposed to the normal or structurally dysfunctional, posture. The technique Master Cai taught us for "eliminating the hollows and protruberances" while standing with the CenterLine perpendicular, was to pull the pelvis and sacrum forward and up while simultaneously slightly pulling in the abdomen. He summarized it in the colorful phrase of "tuck and suck."

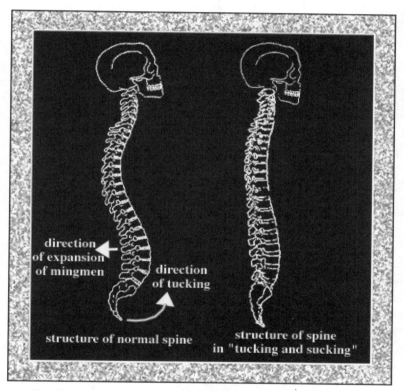

Fig.1.4 Structure of the spine in normal and tucked positions

Tucking the sacrum and sucking in the abdomen lengthens the spine by straightening out its curvatures, particularly the sacral and lumbar curves *(fig 1.4)*. Because the sacrum is dropped down and forward as we "tuck and suck", the lumbar curve is pushed back and straightened out. Master Cai calls this expansion in the small of the lower back "filling the *mingmen* (gate of life)" and he greatly emphasizes the importance of cultivating awareness of this sensation through practice.

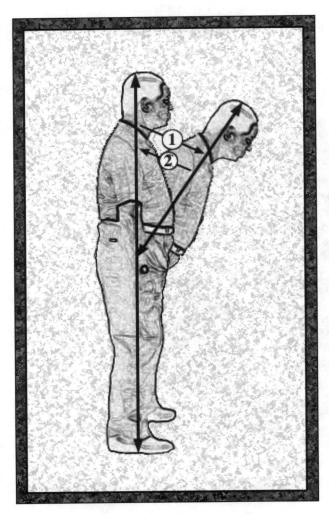

fig. 1.5 Bending forward to get in wuji stance

"Tucking and sucking" adjusts the CenterLine internally by changing the location of the perineum relative to the *baihui (pai hui)* point on the head and the midpoint of the line connecting the bubbling well points on the feet. The resulting realignment of the spine is necessary for the proper transference of weight from the upper part of the torso to the lower at the lumbar-sacral junction and therefore indispensible in reintegrating the lower and upper parts of the torso.

In the beginning at least, the difficulty is that when we do "tuck and suck" in standing position, we automatically tend to tense the hip joints and surrounding musculature, such as the gluteus maximus, even more than we normally do. To help us relax the hips while "eliminating the hollows and protruberances," Master Cai

10

taught us the technique depicted in *fig. 1.5*. After placing feet in parallel position and bending the knees, lean forward slightly from the hips while tucking the pelvis forward and up and sucking the abdomen in. Then maintaining these relationships in lower torso, straighten out slowly and gradually from the hips. Now you will be tucked and sucked while keeping the hips and buttocks relaxed. Once you have learned the sensation of relaxed hips by "sucking and tucking" while bending, then you don't need to bend anymore to get into it .

Biomechanically, the practice of "tucking and sucking" restores the iliopsoas muscles to functionality *(Fig. 1.6)*. This muscle group is one of the most powerful, if least known, of the body's muscles. It connects the spine to the legs and its tonus determines the functionality of the pelvis. Iliopsoatic function is counterbalanced by both the obdurator muscles groups (Todd) and the abdominal muscles groups (Rolf, Heller). When functioning properly in the **natural** state of human affairs, the iliopsoas is instrumental in both walking and sexual activity. Unfortunately, the natural is not the norm.

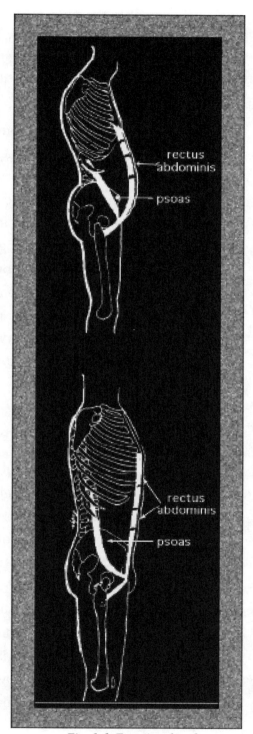

Fig. 1.6 Functional and dysfunctional psoas

In the **normal** state of human affairs, iliopsoatic function is severely impaired, and both the important human activities of walking and sex have become generally dysfunctional. Characteristic of hypertense iliopsoatic dysfunction is the sway back phenomenon, in which the buttocks stick out, and corresponding vicerotopsis, in which the guts appear to be spilling out of the pelvic container (*fig. 1.5a*). Cultivating the habit of "tuck and suck" restores the function of the illopsas, obdurator and abdominal muscle groups and their intimate connection with the diaphragm and the breath. It also restores the container function of the pelvis so that it can actually contain the viscera as it was intended to (*fig 1.5b*). Bear in mind, however, that in the "tuck and suck" formula the tucking is primary, and the sucking secondary. We must learn to suck by tucking. Sucking without tucking is worse than useless.

> In the *taijiquan* classics, the advice for correct posture is to "eliminate the hollows and the protuberances."

Wuji Center As Center Of Gravity

Being mindful of the *wuji* center is both the easiest and most difficult of all meditations. It is easy in the sense that it can be practiced anytime by anyone; you can be in any position, lying still, sitting, standing, walking, otherwise moving. It takes only awareness, not physical energy. So even sick people in hopitals can practice it with great benefit, as Master Cai's work in Traditional Chinese Medicine hospitals has certainly proven. It is difficult because the demands made on us are very strict. "There should be no movement in the body, no movement in the mind, no movement in the intention, and no vision in the eyes."

Chapter 1: Cultivating the CenterPoint

In order to get in touch with our true *wuji* center, it is helpful to summarize the Chinese geography of the lower trunk and the relationship between these four important points: the *dantian*, the *mingmen*, the *huiyin* (perineum) and *wuji* center *(Fig. 1.7)*.

When Master Cai gives the first instructions to beginning students, he always instructs them to "put awareness in the *dantian*", by which he means the general abdomi-

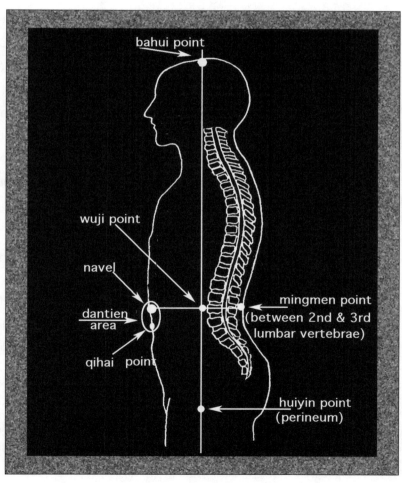

Equalizing the awareness and energy between *dantian* and *mingmen*, front and back, is the precondition for the true location and experience sensation of the *wuji* center proper.

Fig. 1.7 The geography of the lower

nal area around and below the navel. *Dantian* means "field of elixer", after the Taoist and Buddhist discoveries that putting awareness there in meditation generates a warmth and feeling of well being that permeates the entire body. The approximate center of the *dantian* area is the *qi hai* point. approximately 2 inches below the navel.

Second, when the student is ready, Master Cai will instruct her/him to "fill the *mingmen* ". The *mingmen* (gate of life) is the hollowest point in the small of the back, just opposite the *dantian*. It lies on the *dumai (tu mai, tou mei)* channel on the back at the point of integration of the upper and lower parts of the trunk between the 2nd and 3rd lumbar vertebrae. "Filling the *mingmen*" is accomplished by "tucking". Tucking puts awareness in the small of the back and pushes the lower back out, thus eliminating the lumbar curve and straightening the spine. By putting the awareness there, we also put the *qi* (energy) there, thus equalizing the energetic level of the front or *dantian* area and the back or *mingmen* area.

The evolutionary process of human growth is universally recognized as the developmental refinement of grosser physical energies into the subtler energies of mind and spirit.

Equalizing the awareness and energy between *dantian* and *mingmen,* front and back, is the precondition for the true location and experience sensation of the *wuji* center proper. The true *wuji* point, the human center of gravity and biological energy and growth is the point where the line connecting the *dantian* and the *mingmen* intersects the Centerline. This is where we want to focus our awareness. *(fig. 1.7)*

•••

14

Wuji Center As Biological Center

In the Chinese worldview, man is the ultimate fruit which comes from the interaction of the cosmic forces of heaven and earth. We are the central meeting point, the focus in which these two great cosmic forces combine to produce consciousness.

On the purely biological level, a human is like a tree, unfolding in time from its center in the seed, half spiraling downward to root ourselves in the earth and half spiraling upward through the torso to the light, drawing from them and mixing their energies of earth(food,water) and sky(air/light) to fuel organismic growth. In short, the center of gravity is also considered to be the center of biological energy and growth.

The evolutionary process of human growth is universally recognized as the developmental refinement of grosser physical energies into the subtler energies of mind and spirit, a process of gradually merging with the One. In the Chinese tradition, the *jing (ching)*(energy of the lower torso) is said to be refined into *qi* (the energy of the upper torso) which is then refined into *shen* (spirit, or the

Fig. 1.8 Spiral patterns in biological growth

15

energy of the head), which ultimately is refined, or returns to *wu* or nothingness.

The Chinese tradition in general, and the *wuji* tradition in particular, is based on the experience/insight that mindfulness of the center is the way to tap into the very source of the energy that fuels our biological growth. This energy can then be used for purposes of maintaining health and preventing illness, developing martial skills, and spiritual growth.

When our *wuji* center becomes the habitual center of our awareness, we acquire, over time, remarkable experiential abilities of spatial expansion and time dilation.

It is amazing and gratifying to see in how many ways developments in various branches of scientific thought have recently begun to validate many of the basic tenets of this Chinese, particularly Taoist, worldview. Albert Doczi, particularly his book *The Power of Limits,* offers elegant mathematical proof of the basic correctness of the Chinese point of view that the center of gravity in all of life's untold manifestations is also the center of biological energy and growth. In a graphic fashion, Doczi demonstrates how "things grow by the union of complimentary opposites", namely, the *yin* and *yang* of the golden section, the famous pythagorean geometrical formula. His analyses and descriptions show how from the lowly amoeba to the lovely daisy and sunflowers to mighty man, all growth proceeds from the center of the organism and follows the same geometric laws of growth. According to these laws, there is a spiral pattern to biological growth and unfoldment.*(Fig.1.8)* This is all the more interesting because, as we shall see in a later chapter, in the higher levels of accomplishment in *wuji qigong* and *taijiquan* , the human body structure and energy system is also regarded and developed as a spiral structure.

Wuji Center As Center Of Awareness

When our *wuji* center becomes the habitual center of our awareness, we acquire, over time, remarkable experiential abilities of spatial expansion and time dilation.

Kinesthetically, the focusing of awareness on the center in the abdomen is analogous to the focusing of the eyes on a distant object in visual perception. Looking at a distant object with relaxed eyes activates our faculty of peripheral vision which allows us to perceive simultaneously everything in our field of vision. Likewise, by relaxingly centering our awareness in our abdomen, our little-developed sense of peripheral kinesthetic awareness is activated. This allows us to develop simultaneous awareness of the whole body.

When we say that progress in *taijiquan* consists of the growth of body awareness, we refer to this process of making all separate, sequential awarenesses into one simultaneous awareness. In the beginning we must practice each thing separately: We have to make sure our CenterLine is plumb, maintain awareness of the "three points on a straight line" , that the *mingmen* is full, that the components of our foundation are correctly positioned, and the structure of our sphere is properly maintained in all its details.

Because both movement and vision are impediments to developing the awareness of our kinesthetic gestalt, we begin our training in the stillness of *wuji* standing , closing our eyes to shut out the visual component of experience. Then we try to maintain this simultaneous body awareness as we begin to move (slowly) by ourselves with open eyes. Later, we again increase the degree of difficulty when we begin to practice with partners in friendly exchange, in effect, joining with them to form a larger system. Our simultaneous awareness must include not only our own entire body, but also the body of our opponent, and the relative distribution of tension and relaxation within it and between us. As we progress, all the separate little awarenesses become more and more simultaneous to constitute one big awareness embracing all our fields of perception: visual, kinesthetic and auditory. As we train our minds and bodies, these new habits of perception and interaction will become so ingrained as to become our natural responses in times of emergency.

Chapter 2

Cultivating The CenterLine

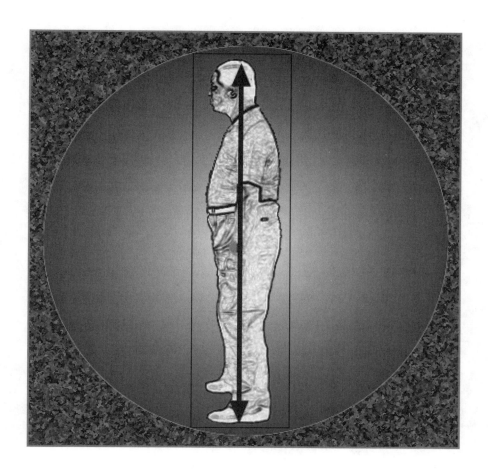

Sinking the *Qi* and Raising the Spirit

Master Cai's optimal postural alignment (and weight distribution) in the *wuji* standing meditation posture are summarized in the phrase "three points on a straight line." These three points that define and constitute the centerline are (1) the perineum, (2) the midpoint of the line connecting the two "bubbling well" points of the feet, and (3) the *baihui* point on the top of the head. *(Fig. 2.1)*

Master Cai was quite specific about the fact that "in standing, nobody can start right away with the centerline as a whole (because) this is the final accomplishment." "The way of getting there," he said, "is to draw, in your mind's eye, a line connecting your navel with the the mingmen point in the small of your back. Then divide this line in half, and again divide each half in half. This gives you five points. Now move your awareness from point one (the navel) to point two then to point three (the centerpoint), then to point four, and then to point five, the mingmen. Then move your awareness back to point four and back to point three, the center point, and keep your awareness there. Once you have located your *wuji* point this way, then connect it first downward to your perineum (the point between the anus and the genitals) and further down to the midpoint of the line connecting bubbling well points of the feet. Then, going the other way, connect the centerpoint upward with the *baihui* point on the head."

This is referred to as sinking the *qi* (into the earth) and raising the spirit (to heaven). The sensation is as if your centerline is being stretched from your centerpoint simul-

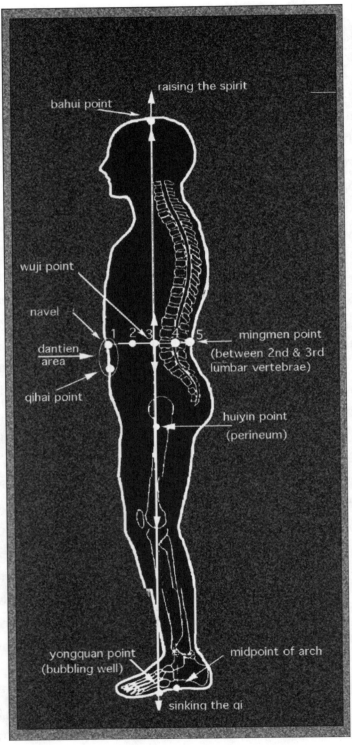

Fig. 2.1 Sinking the Qi and Raising the Spirit

taneously in the direction of heaven, and, in the opposite direction, to the center of the earth. Cultivating awareness of the centerline this way leads to the development of *zhenqi (chen ch'i)*, or control of the centerline energy.

As far as how to circulate the *qi*, you don't have to make the *qi* go anywhere. In fact, if you try to purposely send your energy to a particular place in the body, it may well get stuck at that place. But if you just sink the *qi* and raise the spirit, then the *qi* will flow freely throughout the entire body, filling it with energy that makes it both light and heavy, rooted and agile.

The weight is centered on the bubbling well points on the soles of the feet.

The Foundation

The roots of the human being are in his feet. Our feet are our literal connection to the earth. It is where we make contact, and the quality of that contact deeply affects our awareness of mind and spirit.

The point of contact (feet) both determines and reflects the nature of our posture and quality of balance and equilibrium . It is the point where the exchange of *qi* (energy) between ourselves and the earth takes place.

When Master Cai gives instructions in *wuji qigong* standing meditation, the first thing he always says is to "stand with the feet parallel the width of the shoulder with the knees unlocked," i.e., slightly bent. Then you can "take everything, sink all the energy from the chest on down into the two feet, and thus make contact with the earth in the feet."

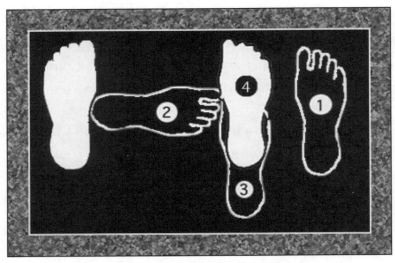

Fig. 2.2 Getting in wuji parellel

The quality of our contact with the earth through our feet affects in a deep way the growth and expansion of our awareness, mind and spirit.

He gave us the following step-by-step method of getting into the *wuji* parallel stance. (1) Start out wide in a roughly parallel, stance. (2) Place the right foot perpendicular to the middle of the left foot. (3) Use the big toe of the right foot as a pivot to swing the right foot into parallel position with the left foot. (4) Finally, advance the right foot forward so that the big toes of both feet touch the same imaginary line. *(Fig. 2.2)*

He insists on the importance of the feet being exactly parallel. If you turn the feet out, he says, the *qi* disperses.

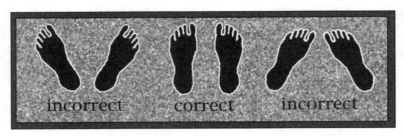

Fig. 2.3 Correct and incorrect positions of the feet

24

On the other hand, if you turn them in(pigeon toed), it will block the smooth flow of the *qi* inside the body and therefore is harmful.*(Fig. 2.3)*

The weight on the feet should be evenly distributed over all the cells of the sole, as if the foot were spreading itself out and grabbing the floor slightly. The weight is on the outside of the feet, the periphery of the circle in which the bubbling well is the central hollow point. This centerpoint will be the last to touch the ground if at all.

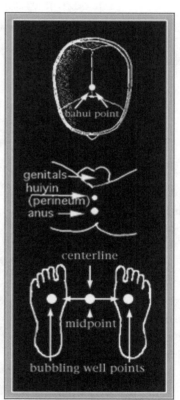

Fig. 2.4. Location of
the three points

As far as the weight distribution from toes to heels, the weight will be slightly forward from center. Particularly in standing meditation, the weight is to be centered on the bubbling well points on the soles of the feet. *(Fig.2.4)* This point is the end and beginning point of the kidney meridian. Actually the bubbling well point is not a point but a hollow located just forward of the arch between the two balls of the feet. It acts like the center of the suction cup when the weight is equally distributed on the periphery of the whole foot. Focussing our weight on those points helps the bad *qi* flow out of the body to be absorbed by the earth as we grow our roots in standing.

The ankle should sit straight on the foot, not leaning either in or out. But whether it does or not depends on the habitual placement of the knees in relation to the feet.

In general, knees tend to bend inward; most people are slightly knock-kneed. This puts weight on the inside of the feet. We must remember to keep knees over toes, as if squeezing an expanding balloon. This will distibute weight evenly over the whole foot. On the other hand, if you have a tendency to be bowlegged, you have to make the

The knees are the fulcrum point of the leg which acts as lever-spring; their position in relation to the two ends of the leg spring, the hips and feet, determine the efficiency of the spring as well as the twisting action of the leg.

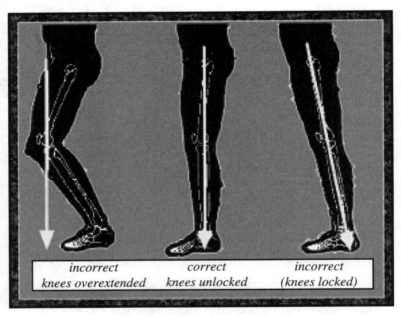

| incorrect | correct | incorrect |
| knees overextended | knees unlocked | (knees locked) |

Fig. 2.5 Alignment of the knees

opposite adjustment. Bowlegged knees put the weight on the outside of the feet. To even it out, squeeze the knees together. This puts more weight on the inside of the feet.

In distributing the pressure of weight on the feet, do not use force. Apply only a slight but steady awareness in the knees. This awareness leads to greater stability and agility.

The knees are the fulcrum point of the leg which acts as lever-spring; their position in relation to the two ends of the leg spring, the hips and feet, determine the efficiency of the spring as well as the twisting action of the leg. The structurally optimal position is with the knees unlocked, slightly bent, plumb over the bubbling well points of the feet. *(Fig. 2.5)*

At first, it is better to have higher stances, with the knees barely unlocked because it will be easier for the *qi* to sink down. In the lower stances, the *qi* will be blocked, because the body has not developed the fundamental strength to be able to relax within the severe demands a lower structure makes; thus tension results and *qi* is blocked. Only very gradually as you build up strength, can you go lower.

The hips are where the weight of the torso is transmitted to the foundation of the legs. The hips must be even. If one is higher than the other, it indicates a lateral curvature of the spine. This creates an inefficient structure which demands excessive energy to maintain. The results will be chronic musculo-fascial blocking and stagnation in the *qi* channels or meridians.

And as Master Cai never tired of reiterating, the hip joints have to be completely relaxed in order for the *qi* (energy) to be able to flow smoothly and sink down into the feet. Then the grounding and centering of the torso can occur.

The hips joints have to be completely relaxed in order for the *qi* (energy) to be able to flow smoothly and sink down into the feet. Then the grounding and centering of the torso can occur.

The Upper Torso

In *wuji qigong* meditation, the arms hang relaxed by the side. In the beginning, they will frequently hang forward in front of the body. But as the shoulders and chest relax over time, they will naturally end up hanging by the side with the middle finger hitting the *fengshi* gall bladder point on the thigh.

Physically, the head is erect on the neck. The chin is tucked down and in slightly so the gaze of the eyes is

Master Cai, following the *taiji* classics, constantly reminded us to "hollow the chest and round the (upper) back."

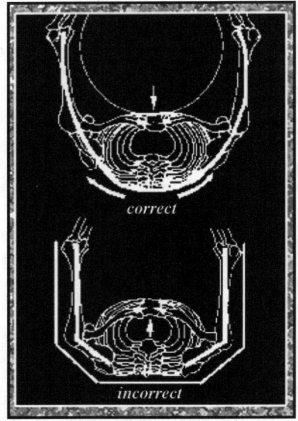

Fig. 2.6 Round the Back and Hollow the Chest

horizontal and in the distance. When you have aligned your body posture along the "three points on a straight line," withdraw your gaze slowly back to the self, closing the eyes as the mental gaze proceeds downward to the *wuji* centerpoint in the abdomen.

The maxim of "eliminating the hollows and protruberances" not only applies to the lower torso but also to the upper part of the torso. Our normal, habitually dysfunctional postural habit is for the chest to be tensed and stuck out by means of the shoulders being pulled back. To rectify this situation, Master Cai, following the *taiji* classics, constantly reminded us to "hollow the chest and round the (upper) back" by relaxing the shoulders, letting them drop downward and forward. As clearly shown in *Fig 2.6*, in the habitual incorrect posture, both the sternum and the rib cage push out, which results in the arms not being fully connected with the scapulae. On the other hand when both the sternum and the ribcage are sunk in slightly, the properly rounded connection of the arms with the scapulae is obtained. Hence "round the back and hollow the chest."

Following the classics, Master Cai put great emphasis on "pulling up the spine" and "raising the spirit". The result of this postural intention of *hankung babei (han kung pa pei)*, pulling up the spine, will be to loosen the vertebral joints, thereby allowing the energy to rise up along the spine. This helps to relax the chest and upper back and achieves the hollowing of the chest and the rounding of the back, which in turn will enable us to effortlessly release or discharge our inner energy from the

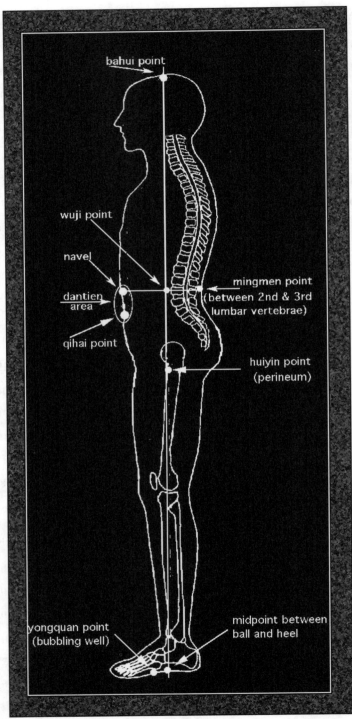

Fig. 2.7 Centerline grounding point in advanced standing

point between the shoulder blades when needed in martial arts use.

Closely connected with pulling up the spine is the habit of "raising the spirit". In the classics, it is variously described as "putting the light and sensitive energy on top of the head", or "feeling as though suspended from the sky by a string", or "feeling as though you're carrying a bucket of water on top of the head." "In this way", Master Cai said, "you raise the spirit (awareness) by connecting your centerpoint upward to the *baihui* point on your skull."

Advanced Standing and Closing Practice

There are several subtle, but important differences between the instructions Master Cai gives to students just beginning their standing meditation practice and those who have been practicing for a while.

First, when you begin your standing meditation practice, the bottom points of the "three points on a line" centerline is between the bubbling well point. This allows the stagnant *qi* to drain from your body into the ground at the bubbling well points in the feet, which are the end points of the kidney meridians. In more advanced stages the point where the centerline enters the ground is moved back to the midpoint of the line connecting the two points halfway between the balls of the feet and the heels in order to give you the most optimal physiologically stable posture. *(Fig. 2.7)*

Fig. 2.8 Closing the meditation with bended wrists

Fig. 2.9 Rubbing eyes

Chapter 2 Cultivating the CenterLine

Secondly, as you progress in *wuji* standing, your base (the width of the feet) becomes smaller, and you can make your practice stance narrower. In the beginning the feet are placed apart as wide as the shoulders. As you become more advanced, the width of your stance will gradually narrow to become as wide as the inside of your shoulders, i. e., the width of the body cylinder . Making the base narrower increases the difficulty of staying still and stable.

Third, while initially the knees are bent somewhat., as you advance, your stance will become even higher to the point where the knees are almost completely straight and just barely unlocked.

Fourth, in the beginning you may lean or incline the centerline forward slightly to give greater grounding because of the centerline structure being pushed into the ground. As you advance, you will keep the centerline perfectly plumb and vertical, because a plumb centerline is narrower in diameter then an inclining centerline and is therefore more easily maneuverable and more difficult for an opponent to control and move.

As a closing practice for your standing exercise, bend the wrists at the hip level for one to two minutes. Master Cai says this practice will help to get rid of any bad *qi* you may have accumulated during your meditation.*(Fig. 2.8)* But, he advises, don't do it too long, because you will lose your good *qi* too. Now, slowly open your eyes, taking in infinity, and rub your face with the palms of your hands.*(Fig. 2.9)*

Chapter 3

Wuji Qigong As Healing Art

The Chinese View

What follows are certain remarks, some abridged and some amplified, made by Master Cai on the health benefits to be derived from the practice of *wuji qigong*. These remarks are taken from a talk he gave on December 14, 1984 at the School of Traditional Chinese Medicine in San Francisco, where he is an honorary lecturer.

According to the Chinese theory of medicine, the whole life system depends on *zhenqi* or the "true *qi*" When the "true *qi*" is in abundance, the health is good. When the true *qi* is deficient, the body is weak. When the true *qi* disappears, life ends. As a result of this world view, *qigong* developed as a practice and life style—a conscious longevity strategy to (re)generate "true *qi*" in order to heal our illnesses and strengthen our weaknesses, thus delaying the day our portion of "true *qi*" is exhausted and we die.

> **One of the greatest benefits accrued through *qigong* practice is the strengthening of the immune and other defensive systems of the body.**

One of the greatest benefits accrued through *qigong* practice is the strengthening of the immune and other defensive systems of the body. By maximizing the immune and other defense systems, *qigong* practice effectively maintains health and cures sickness. By promoting efficient circulation of the "true *qi*"through all the meridians, *qigong* practice increases the supply of life force to all the cells of the body, thus increasing efficiency of the whole body.

Moreover, the effects of *qigong* pratice are not limited to healing ourselves. We can go beyond that and through *qigong* practice develop a special kind of strength, a strength of the ligaments and bones of the body, thus increasing physical strength and stamina. It also has great beneficial effects to our nervous system, and our perceptual and intellectual functions are stimulated for maximum development.

By aligning the "three points on a straight line," abundant true *qi* will be generated in the *wuji* centerpoint.

In *wuji qigong*, we align our posture in accordance with the principle of "three points on a straight line" and concentrate our consciousness in the navel area. In this position, abundant "true *qi*" can be generated in the wuji centerpoint and from there flow up and down the centerline and the main meridians, in turn opening up all the other meridians. The principle of "three points on a straight line", guarantees that the centerline is plumb, resulting in the proper alignment of the spine. By "filling the mingmen," or straightening the curve of the lumbar spine, the lower back is expanded, which allows the *qi* (energy) to flow freely up and down the spine. With "three points on a straight line," the centerline is unobstructed, the body is integrated and non-segmented. In any other position of the spine, the centerline is broken and the *qi* cannot flow freely; the body is posturally disintegrated, and health problems will likely result.

The wuji center in the *dantian* area is the fountainhead of the "true *qi*." Before birth, a fetus receives true *qi* through the umbilical cord along with all the nutrition necessary for the growth of the cells. After the umbilical cord is severed, the external *qi* from the air comes in through the mouth and nostrils. We call it post natal *qi*. The prenatal *qi* continues to reside in the *dantian* area near the navel. The wuji center as biological center also coincides with the location of our center of gravity, which is essential for the balance and equilibrium of the body.

In the *wuji* system of *qigong*, after concentrating on this area for days or months or years, the true *qi* will burst, fill up the *dantian* and then, step by step, open up all the meridians. As a physical manifestation of this process, frequently a wonderfully warm feeling in the abdominal area radiates throughout the entire body. The practice of *wuji qigong* is totally safe and will not have any adverse side effects. By cultivating a great amount of true *qi* and circulating it throughout the body, *wuji qigong* prevents the stagnation of *qi* in the meridians or the accumulation of unhealthy *qi* in local tissues.

In *wuji qigong,* we use the technique of focusing attention in the *wuji* center behind the navel in order to generate the true *qi* and open up all the meridians.

After you have practiced for a suffcent time, the cultivation of "true *qi*"will develop many other fascinating abilitites. First as your meridians open up and the "true *qi*" flows through them abundantly, you will develop awareness of the circulation of the flow of energy through your own meridians. In time, this growing awareness and sensitivity will extend outward and you will also be able to feel and understand the energy and meridian system of someone else. Then the stage is set for a healing exchange. Standing next to the recipient, the practitioner uses his awareness to lock the signal of his own energy system in phase with the energy system of the patient, enabling him

In time, this growing awareness and sensitivity will extend outward and you will also be able to feel and understand the energy and meridian system of someone else. Then the stage is set for a healing exchange.

(1) to monitor the energy defects of the patient and (2) to allow his own energy to flow into the patient to help him/her reinforce and reestablish *qi* balance.

Questions and Answers

During his two stays in the U.S., Master Cai conducted numerous workshops introducing his *wuji qigong* practice to the American public. What follows are some of the most-asked questions during these sessions. His answers further elucidate how the practice of *wuji qigong* harmonizes with and is premised on the model of the human body/mind of Traditional Chinese Medicine and philosophy.

Question: I felt pain and discomfort in my shoulders. Does that mean the energy was blocked there?

40

The feeling of discomfort is your first awareness of blockage there...usually, the weakest part of us will register discomfort first.

Answer: Yes, the feeling of discomfort is your first awareness of blockage there. Before, you trained yourself to ignore it by tensing and contracting. Relaxing it a little brings it to the threshold of awareness and thus is the first step. Usually, the weakest part in us will register discomfort first; it is different for everyone.

Question: I find that the constant pressure on both feet while standing makes it hard to keep the meridians along the bottom open, and I become numb.

Answer: There is no way to avoid it in the beginning. When acquiring any new skill, you can expect to have some growing pains. The solution is to gradually increase the length of your standing practice. Then the body will adjust and feeling and sensation will not diminish, but increase.

Question: I'm feeling queasy and sick to my stomach after standing. Why is that?

Answer: Well, that's the part of your body that is deficient in *qi* and where there is a problem; therefore, when you haven't stood long enough and you try to summon the *qi*, it will be weak and not yet able to break through the blocks in the meridians. And that creates the discomfort. So as you practice your discomfort will gradually decrease until, postively, you experience a type of ecstasy.

Question: How do you gauge the seriousness of a *qi* blockage?

Answer: By the degree of discomfort and the loss of functionality. When *qi* is blocked, small blockage will manifest as discomfort at first, larger blockages as pain, even larger as chronic disease such as cancer. Finally, total blockage, or total absence of the flow of *qi*, is death.

Question: I get very sleepy while doing standing meditation

Answer: Well, if you're tired, just walk around a little, or take a rest. As you practice, at first when you relax, you may want to go to sleep; but later when you relax, you become more and more alert and awake. That is the process.

Question: I find it difficult to keep my awareness in the *dantian* because my mental component is going so strongly. What can I do?

Answer: It takes time to learn the habit of relaxation. So just be patient with yourself and persevere, and when the awareness wanders, just bring it back to the center.

Question: My hands get warmer and there's a lot of

> As you practice, your discomfort will gradually decrease until, postively, you experience a type of ecstasy.

spontaneous movement in my fingers

Answer: Good, your *qi* is working

Question: I notice that by just standing, my circulation increases

Answer: In Traditional Chinese Medicine blood and *qi* are always considered to go together. In our practice when the *qi* starts to flow and circulate, the blood comes right along with it, and it is because of that that healing takes place.

Question: In breathing, does it matter whether you breathe through your nose or your mouth?

Answer: Naturally, through the nose if you can because it will filter out impurities from the air. Of course if you have nose problems, then by all means breathe in through the mouth.

Question: When you were adjusting me, were you trying to get me to hold my stomach in a little bit?

Answer: I was trying to do what we call "harmonizing the body" by making certain adjustments and putting you in the right posture, so that your belly isn't hanging out and your buttocks aren't sticking out. This I call "suck (the abdomen) and tuck" (the buttocks and pelvis). In the beginning it may feel a little artificial and strained, but again you must develop certain musculature before it can begin to feel natural.

> When the *qi* starts to flow and circulate, the blood comes right along with it, and it is because of that that healing takes place.

Question: Should I try to take deep breaths?

Answer: No, do not try to take deep breaths. You allow yourself to breathe naturally, just like you're talking or whatever. Don't put any intention in it, only pay attention to it.

Question: After the first several minutes, my legs

started to shake uncontrolably. And then when I focused my awareness in the abdominal area, everything went numb.

...one of the advantages large group meditations is that the energy of the group can be used to speed up certain developmental processes.

Answer: This indicates a weakness in the lower part of the body which is not as strong as the other part. Also because we have many people here, a very strong field is generated which may be acting to catalyze your reactions. This is actually one of the advantages of working in large groups doing meditation; the energy of the group can be

used to speed up certain developmental processes.

Question: I too experienced tremendous shaking and bouncing.

Answer: Let me draw an anology with plumbing. Your meridians are like the water pipes. When they are kinked or blocked, the water pressure may set off vibrations and shaking in the pipes. Same with the *qi*; different blockages have different effects, shaking and bouncing are among them.

Question: What is the relationship of sitting to standing meditation?.

Answer: Well, each is a different path to mindfulness, and once you've reached mindfulness all the time, the path you took to get there no longer matters. Besides that, each have their reason for doing what they do. Standing is of course much more demanding than sitting, so certainly if you don't have the strength to do standing, you just do sitting. The reason we stand is to cultivate awareness of (1) how the center sits still on the root and (2) how the center is made mobile by the root. Besides promoting health, standing practice has deep implications for agility and stability in martial arts.

Question: What does it mean when you're standing and your arms have a sensation that they want to float up?

Answer: The *qi* will be flowing in you according to where it needs to go. If when you 're standing and keeping awareness centered in the abdomen and the hands want to rise, just let them rise, but do not put intention in them. Often times raising the hands has to do with the redistribution of equilibrium, for as the *qi* increases it may change your balance distribution as well. That may be a factor.

Question: Why is it better to stand than to move?

Answer: If you have injury in the body and blockage in the meridians, you don't have enough *qi* in the body to heal yourself when you're moving because you're using energy when you're moving. Movement is already directing the *qi*, as the classics say. We believe that the *qi* must first be generated in stillness so it will naturally well up and circulate. Then, it can be used in movement and can be

> The *qi* must first be generated in stillness so it will naturally well up and circulate. Then, it can be used in movement and can be directed.

WUJI QIGONG AND THE ESSENCE OF TAIJIQUAN

directed. Particularly as we get older, the main job is always to generate the *qi* and develop our mental abilities, and not to deplete our energy thru excessive use of movement.

Question: So, if you're swaying or otherwise moving, should you allow that and enjoy it or should you stop it with your mind?

Answer: Yes, keep the center still. Your body is affected by the flow of *qi*, so movement is often the result of a weakness or imbalance of *qi*. Again, just maintain your stillness and your center, then the *qi* will go where it is needed to heal and not be drained in involuntary movement.

Question: It appears standing meditation is the absolute key and the movement is built on top of it?

Answer: Yes, *taiji* comes from wuji, as the classics say, so this is the appropriate way of cultivating and using *qi*. In wuji meditation we learn to control our movement by gaining control of the stillness at our center. Otherwise put, to control your center, you must be still in body and mind. Thus, mindfulness of the center leads to true mastery of movement.

as much as you can, avoid thinking because it is verbal and linear. Do increase and seek awareness, which is non verbal and simultaneous.

Question: Why do you have us put our weight on the bubbling well points and not the heel?

Answer: We keep our centerline awareness in the bubbling well points of the feet so that the bad *qi* can leave the body there. The bubbling well points are the end points of the kidney meridian; putting weight on them aids the discharge of the bad *qi* at these points. This is what we want, first of all, so this is what we do. Putting the weight on the heel may develop a particular kind of strength or

46

whatever, but it makes it harder for us to get rid of the bad *qi*. So it is always what you want to cultivate that determines your practice. Other people may try to achieve different things by emphasing other things.

Question: You said there should be no thought during meditation?

Answer: Yes, as much as you can, avoid thinking because it is verbal and linear. Do increase and seek awareness, which is non verbal and simultaneous. You're not asked to become numb or to dim awareness. On the contrary, you must observe within yourself. That is how you gain the knowledge and learn how the *qi* really works.

Question: When you have some discomfort, is it better to relieve it by moving it a little bit, or do you try not to move and allow it to work itself out somehow?

Answer: Yes, don't move, if you can help it; if you can't help it, just let it happen. Either way, don't make a big deal about it.

Question: How should we deal with physical or emotional urges that may come up during standing?

Answer: When you stand, it is important when things begin to happen to let them happen. If you burp or fart or your hands get cold or hot, you want to cry or shake, let it happen; don't repress it; it is negative *qi* getting out

Question: Do we use our mind and attention to direct the *qi,* the energy to that part of the body we seek to heal, or does the *qi* energy just go there naturally?

Answer: This is a very common question. In our practice we concentrate, focus awareness on the navel area to generate the true *qi* there. When it develops, it will, of its own accord, suffuse and permeate throughout the

Intentional focusing of awareness on the affected areas themselves can actually be a hindrance to healing...In our practice we focus awareness on the navel area to generate the true *qi* there.

body in general and particularly the areas that are affected. We allow it but do not use intention to guide it,. We believe that intentional focusing of awareness on the affected areas themselves can actually be a hindrance to

healing. At first you may get some apparent benefits, but the later side effects are not worth it. We

just try to activate the natural process, and then allow the wisdom of the body to direct its own battle against the imbalances. As an example, if you think of the body as a balloon and the mind as the pump and the valve that pumps up the air in the balloon, it has to be done slowly and carefully; if you focus the air too strongly and quickly, you may burst a balloon at its weakest part; instead you must seek to strengthen the weaker part slowly.

Question: How is *wuji qigong* used in the Chinese

Our practice is more interested in opening up all our own meridians to heal ourselves with our *qi*, not to gain control over people or things that are external to us.

hospitals where you work? What kind of conditions is it used on?

Answer: On every sickness. For example, if you have an operation on your stomach, then after the operation, they will start you right away doing *wuji qigong* to help you regenerate the energy and speed natural healing,

Question: Can you force the power of the *qi* on people or anything?

Answer: Our practice is more interested in opening up all our own meridians to heal ourselves with our *qi*, not to gain control over people or things that are external to us. Those may be side effects , so to speak, but cannot be the primary objective, for if your motivation is power, you've already failed. If it happens, it happens. It's not important.

Question: Is *wuji qigong* used in psychiatric hopsitals or wards?

We put awareness on the centerpoint so the *qi* will generate in the belly . When the center is full, and the centerline is truly plumb and open the *qi* begins to overflow and circulate up and down in the centerline and the other meridians.

Answer: Generally, it is used more with sober-minded people. With people who are afflicted in the head, it is difficult to have results; they are so much in their heads while we are in the body. At that point psychiatrists are needed more; *qigong* practice may actually exacerbate or worsen their connditions if carried out without strict supervision.

Question: Surprisingly, my experience was that the standing was much much easier and enjoyable during the second time we did it.

Answer: Of course, everything gets easier and more pleasurable through repetition. Practice makes perfect!

Question: Could you say more about the relationship of both the health and the martial arts aspects of *wuji qigong* practice?

Answer: There is a wonderful unity in the way in which the theory and practice of Central Equilibrium in *wuji qigong* accomplishes its twin aims of first promoting health and vitality and second improving martial ability.

The principle of *wuji qigong* is that the practice of optimum posture promotes optimum health. We put awareness on the centerpoint so the *qi* will generate in the belly. When the center is full and the centerline is truly plumb and open, the *qi* begins to overflow and circulate up and down in the centerline and the other meridians. Therefore meditation on the centerline, i.e., postural meditation, is the key to the proper ciculation of the *qi* through the entire body where the *qi* can do its healing work, breaking down the blockages and strenthening weak areas. The skill of *wuji qigong* and Central Equilibrium utilizes the mind to suffuse all parts of the body with

"Don't worry about the breath, just put awareness in the center (in the abdomen) and breathe naturally, to the point where you forget that you are breathing at all."

50

qi.

Awareness of the center and centerline is also the key to success in martial arts use. Obviously, Central Equilibrium plays the most profound role in pushhands and martial arts application. At the highest level, you are able to deal with the attack of several people at the same time even when standing on one foot. In martial arts and pushhands competition, if you lose Central Equilibrium, you have lost.

Thoughts on the Breath and Breathing

Under the influence of the widespread proliferation of breath-oriented *qigong* practices in the past few decades, a debate regarding the role of the breath and breathing in *taijiquan* has been ongoing in the *taijiquan* community. On the one hand, there is the experimentally oriented faction which has enthusiastically incorporated *qigong*-type breath control practices into their *taijiquan* practice. These advocates of conscious breathing argue that to consciously cultivate deep natural abdominal breathing and harmonize it with the *taiji* movements is indispensible if we want to achieve functional body integration. On the other hand, the more traditionally oriented masters and practicioners have continued to insist that *qigong* type breathing practices have no place in the practice of *taijiquan* . Most of those opposed to the cultivation of the breath say it is not necessary. They argue that just doing the *taiji* movement will automatically and naturally harmonize the breath with it and do its integrative work.

During the exhalation phase of the natural breathing cycle, the deepest total body relaxation coincides with the greatest functional integration of the upper and lower parts of the torso.

51

Master Wu Daye (Wu Ta Yeh) from Palo Alto, California., has been a particularly eloquent exponent of the traditionalist view. The late great grandmaster Zheng Manqing also held to this view when he said that in *taiji* practice "breathing is not a conscious act. It is not forcing the air down. It is keeping the heart/mind focused on the *dantian* that leads the air there". (Lowenthal, p.98) Master Cai also holds this opinion. Whenever he was asked questions concerning the role of the breath, he always responded by saying "Don't worry about it (the breath), just put awareness in the center (in the abdomen) and breathe naturally, to the point where you forget that you are breathing at all."

The centers of gravity, growth, movement and breath all coincide in one point, our *wuji* center.

As a contribution to this ongoing discussion, I'd like to present here my own experience of the use of the breath in wuji and *taiji* practice. You might say I've come full circle with it, going from not paying attention to it to paying a lot of attention to it, back to not paying attention. When I first learned *taijiquan* with Master Ha , no particular attention was paid to the breath. We were told not to worry about it, just learn the movements and the breath would follow naturally. And indeed, as the *taiji* movements became a more integral part of my being, I became aware of how the breath naturally harmonized with my movements. I then discovered the conscious use of the breath to be a very efficient tool in the process of reintegrating the upper and lower parts of my body. Under the influence of Master Cai, I further evolved from being an exponent of the modern position of "using the breath to integrate the body" back into a practitioner of the traditionalist point of view "integrate the body and the breath will follow."

My "middle period," so to speak, when I emphasized the conscious cultivation of my breath, was the result of an insight that there is a important distinction between normal and natural breathing. Up to that point, most of my breathing had been normal breathing, centered in the chest and involving only the upper torso. I realized that this normal breathing is not natural breathing. Natural breathing involves the lower as well as the upper part of the torso, the pelvis, abdomen and lower part of the spine as well as the chest. Both through academic research and personal experience, I discovered that in natural breathing, the exhalation is particularly important. In it the deepest total body relaxation coincides with the greatest functional integration of the upper and lower parts of the torso.

Only when the *qi* is equal at the *mingmen* and the *dantian*, will it truly reside in the *wuji* center from where it can go up and down the centerline, or center tube of energy.

Biomechanically, in abdominally centered exhalation (1) the pelvis tucks under forward and up, (2) the abdominal muscles contract and the abdomen and stomach are sucked in and up, and (3) the lower back in general, and the *mingmen* (gate of life) expands and is "filled up". These simultaneous actions serve to integrate the body into a functional unit. Experientially, in natural breathing, the *wuji* point is the origin and destination of each breath. The expansion (inflation) of the torso on the inhale begins in the abdomen and rises to include the chest. The contraction or deflation of the torso begins in the chest and descends down again in the abdomen... Thus, the centers of gravity, growth, movement and

53

breath all coincide in one point, our wuji center.

Yet, when I met Master Cai I soon learned that he also does not believe in cultivating the breath to achieve integration. "Don't worry about the breath", he kept repeating, "just breathe naturally and focus your awareness in your wuji center". This puzzled me for some time. I did not understand how he could ignore such an obviously efficient method to achieve body integration. It was not until I practiced doing it his way for a few years that the answer came to me: Master Cai in effect bypasses the breath. His method uses *yi*, awareness or intention, directly to achieve integration. That Master Cai's method has to be at least twice as fast in producing results can be easily demonstrated. On the other hand, it may be twice as difficult. The basic view is that we know that the right posture of maximum integration is the posture of exhalation. So you use the mind to maintain a constant posture of exhalation through the entire breathing cycle, including the inhalation. This is exactly what the ancient formula "eliminate the hollows (lower back)and protuberances (abdomen)", more colorfully expressed by Master Cai as "suck and tuck" amounts to. By tucking the pelvis under, forward and up and sucking the abdomen in, the (lumbar) spine in the lower back is pushed out , the mingmen (gate of life) is filled up and the torso is integrated.

In natural breathing, the belly is fully extended on the inhale and contracted on exhale. Master Cai's method is to keep the abdomen sucked and the pelvis tucked at all times, even in inhalation. The reason, says Master Cai, is

*Within the constancy of this exhalation posture, the breath will naturally be centered in the *wuji* center of integration where the *yi* (intention) is already focused.*

54

that if you let all the *qi* go forward, as in natural breathing when the belly extends, then it won't go to the back; i.e. it will detract from the mingmen and disintegrate the body at the mingmen. By keeping the pelvis tucked constantly, the *qi* is kept at the mingmen, integrating the body even during inhalation. Only when the *qi* is equal at the *mingmen* and the *dantian*, will it truly reside in the wuji center from where it can go up and down the centerline, or center tube of energy.

Thus it becomes evident that when we use the breathing method to promote integration, the body is actually integrated only half the time, during the exhalation. With the use of *yi*, or mindfulness, for integration, the posture is held continuously, twice as long, while maintaining the sensation of the breath sinking down into the wuji center on the exhale and rising up into the chest on the inhale. Within the constancy of this exhalation posture, the breath will naturally be centered in the wuji center of integration where the yi (awareness/intention) is already focused. Just put your mind to it, your determination and willpower. And above all, relax. Even from the point of view of those advocating focused awareness on breathing as integrative function, it must be admitted that the practice on constant tucking makes sense. If the posture of exhalation is the posture of integration, the posture of inhalation is the posture of segmentation (disintegration). Master Cai's method of awareness keeps the body in a constantly integrated state, irregardless of inhalation or exhalation; the segmentation part of the breathing cycle is

The very relationship of the human organism to its environment is fundamentally mediated by the functional polarity of the sympathetic and parasympathetic nervous systems.

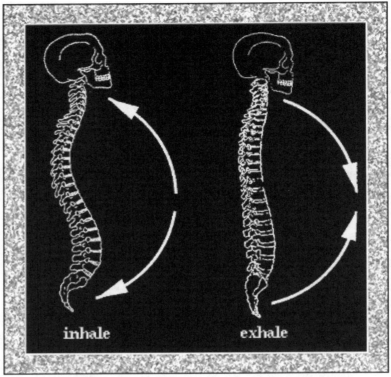

Fig. 3.1 Undulation of spine in natural breathing cycle

avoided, and progress towards integration doubled.

Personally, I practice Master Cai's method. But I have found in my own teaching that with beginning students it is highly beneficial to teach them the conscious use of the breath. When people first start learning, the lumbar spine, pelvis and abdomen are often so frozen and locked in position that giving them instructions to maintain "tuck and suck" constantly only increases the general level of tension and inability to feel in the area. They will be unable to originate and return the breath to the wuji center. The rhythmic process of exertion in tucking and sucking on the exhale and nonexertion of extending the belly and the swing back of the pelvis on the inhale represents the *undulation of spine in natural breathing cycle.(Fig. 3.1)* Practicing it enables students to locate the origin and destination of the breath in the wuji center, and is the only way to activate the musculature so they start having feeling and sensations in the area. Once this has been accomplished they can fruitfully maintain the "suck and tuck" postural demands solely with the yi or mindful intention.

A Western Rationale

Life oscillates between states of relative harmony and emergency of the organism with its environment. Indeed, the very relationship of the human organism to its environment is fundamentally mediated by the functional polarity of the sympathetic and parasympathetic nervous systems. The sympathetic nervous system is the backbone of the human neurophysiology of emergency. As a system, it marshalls the existing resources of our organisms to deal with external threats by activating the pituitary-adrenal system. This enables us to deal with immediate threats and states of emergency, either by flight or fight. Stimulation of the parasympathtic nervous system, on the other hand, is accompanied by feelings of expansion and turgor with the secretion of endorphines. Under conditions of harmony or oneness with the environment, pleasure and joy rather than fear or anger, are the operant and characteristic emotions. The breathing cycle also reflects this basic polar structure: the parasympathtic nervous system is

Meditation gives us the tools to change our current habitual state of stress and emergency into one of harmony.

stimulated on the exhale, while the sympathteic nervous system is stimulated on the inhale.

The practice of "raising the spirit and sinking the *qi*" mimic and reinforce basic mammalian response patterns to emergency situations.

Using these categories, we can better begin to understand what Master Cai means when he talks about the "purpose of wuji standing meditation is the cultivation of the "true *qi*", as the source of preventive self-care and restorative healing processes. In Chinese traditonal medicine and meditative practices, the "true *qi* " is closely related to the pursuit of "prenatal *qi*," or the energy state of the infant before birth. From this, it is not difficult to see why the ancient (and modern) alchemists and meditators would so highly value the pursuit of prenatal and true *qi* while devaluing postnatal *qi*, the predominant energy state of the human being after birth. The Chinese pursuit of prenatal or "true *qi* " is nothing but the attempt to create that kind of energy flow within our bio-psychic system which is like the relationship of the organism to the environment in the womb. That is to say, a condition where the psychophysiology of emergency is deactivated in order to maximize process of growth and nourishment. Put in western terminlogy, the pursuit of prenatal or true *qi* is the attempt to maximize the operation of the physio-psychology of harmony. It is cultivating that state of the

human organism in which our body, mind and spirit is at one with our natural, social, and cosmic environment.

It is equally clear that after birth, the relationship between organism and environment is radically altered. The harmony of the prenatal period, is over and a new polarity begins. At best, harmony now fluctuates with emergency. At worst, the state of emergency becomes chronic and habitual. The environment becomes larger and more dangerous. Thus the postnatal *qi* of the organism after birth refers to that state of energy and being characterized by the functioning of psycho-phsyiology of emergency, in which the organism finds itself at odds with the environment and, draining its resources, must expend energy away from growing and into self defense.

Both the tragedy and dilemma of modern humanity is that it has internalized the psychophysiology of emergency, flight and fight, on a global scale.

Both the tragedy and dilemma of modern humanity is that it has internalized the psychophysiology of emergency, flight and fight, on a global scale. In the biological, psychological, spiritual, political, social and economic structures and institutions, humankind is mindlessly ruled by fear and aggression, creating a self-perpetuating and self-feeding emergency situation spiraling out of control and draining the psychological and physical energy reserves both of the human individual and humanity as a whole. Only stillness can provide the antidote within the person and within the civilization. Only meditation gives us the tools to change our current habitual state of stress and emergency into one of harmony. Thus the practice of meditation, in general, takes on immense relevance for humanity, giving us the ability to control our physiological and psychological states through relaxation.

The particular uniqueness and relevance of wuji standing, as we shall see in the course of this book, is that it makes accessible to us the emergency powers of the body while remaining in a state of harmony. In the martial dimension, we reclaim the emergency powers of our mammalian heritage without our organism being overwhelmed or governed by them.

We described in some detail how Master Cai's practice of "raising the spirit and sinking the *qi*" changes our normal/civilized bodies and enables us to regain our natural/instinctive posture and movement. For indeed the practice of "raising the spirit and sinking the *qi*" mimic and reinforce basic mammalian response patterns to emergency situations.

Raising the head and the spirit refers to the alertness response which activates the sensory-neural apparatus and integrates it with the neuro-muscular system. Sinking the *qi* refers to bodily mobilization which activates the "crouch" response. The tucking under of tailbone and

> Raising the head and the spirit refers to the alertness response which activates the sensory-neural apparatus and integrates it with the neuro-muscular system. Sinking the *qi* refers to bodily mobilization which activates the "crouch" response.

60

pelvis, expanding the lower back and filling the mingmen integrates the upper and lower bodies, making their combined power available to deal with emergency situations.

By "keeping three points on a straight line" and "sinking the *qi* and raising the spirit", *wuji* meditation cultivates a state of awareness/being in stillness that may best be described as the perpetual "calm before the storm," the stillness and heightened awareness of the cat that precedes its jump on its prey. The goal of *wuji* meditation is to acquire the strength of calm so that the storm never breaks, the total alertness and readiness to "jump the prey" without ever jumping. By maximizing cultivation and minimizing use, *wuji* meditation generates the true *qi,* i.e. increases our energy potential and accesses our human emergency powers while continuing to operate under the psychophysiology of harmony.

PART II
BEING MINDFUL OF THE FOUNDATION AND SPHERE
HOW TO CULTIVATE AWARENESS OF
RELAXATION AND INTEGRATION FOR MARTIAL ARTS

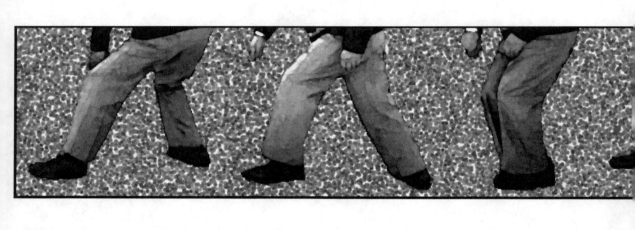

Chapter 4.

Cultivating The Foundation

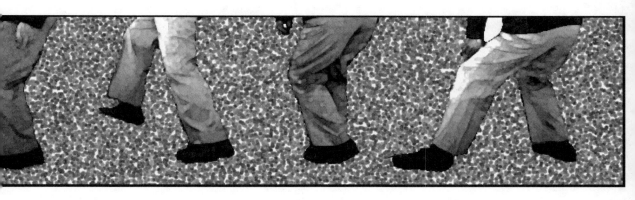

Archer Step

In *wuji qigong* meditation the emphasis is on keeping the centerline still. In *taiji qigong* meditation, the emphasis is on the movement of the centerline. Before discussing the possible movements of the centerline, we must understand how to provide an adequate foundation of legs and feet. The more stable the foundation structure, the more stable the centerline will be in its movement. Therefore, the legs must be strenthened to provide the most secure structure by which the centerline can move. In training for this, you start with stillness which leads to integration which later enables you to move with integration. Then you have stillness within movement.

> It is axiomatic that the more stable the foundation structure, the more stable the centerline will be in its movement.

This job of "building the foundation", as Master Cai put it, is carried out primarlly in the basic *taiji* stance of the archer step in which one foot is in front of the other as opposed to the parellel stance of *wuji* meditation. "Building the foundation" is extremely hard work that pays off and lives up to its promise, as anyone who puts in the time to follow Master Cai's meticulously detailed instructions will find out.

To begin with, said Master Cai, consider that if your step is too narrow, then you will be very stable forward and backward, but very unstable sideways. Conversely, if you have a wider stance you will be very stable sideways, and very unstable forward and backward. Therefore, when in the archer step, your step should be neither too long nor too wide.

Start from *wuji* parallel stance, feet shoulder width apart. Narrow the distance between the feet to where it is one fist wide. This makes your feet line up properly with the hips and shoulders and optimizes the body's balance and maintains control over the centerline. Turn the right foot out 45 degrees and advance the left foot 2 1/2 to 3 ft. The fist-width distance between the feet creates what we call "the channel" *(Fig.4.1)*. Exactly how far you step depends on your ability, that is the relative tightness or looseness of your hips. You must experiment and find the right balance between the extremes. Do not overextend yourself, for then your hips will not be stable; on the other hand, if you make your stance too small, you won't get the real benefit of the exercise.

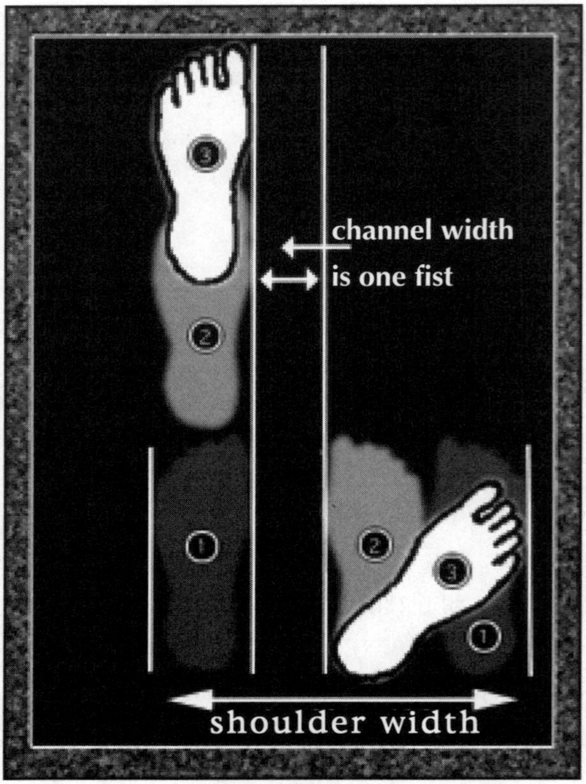

Fig. 4.1 Getting into archer stance

Do not overextend yourself, for then your hips will not be stable; on the other hand, if you make your stance too small, you won't get the real benefit of the exercise.

Visualize the distance from the toe of the front foot to the heel of the rear foot and divide it into four equal parts. This gives you five points of reference. In postures, you will be in the most comfortable position at the center point no. 3. Point no. 3 is midpoint between no.1 and point no.5. Point no.4 is midpoint between point no.3 and point no.5; point no.2 is midpoint between point no.1 and point no.3. *(Fig. 4.2)*

68

Chapter 4 Being Mindful of the Foundation

In the archer step, as in the parallel stance, most of the work is done with the centerline positioned plumb over the third, central point. In fact it is the bottom point of the "three points on a straight line" idea discussed in Chapter 3. So pay attention and be comfortable around your third point. This is your optimal point and will demonstrate the greatest effects in martial arts application. Therefore in *wuji qigong*, the emphasis is primarily on how to cultivate stability and structure around the centerpoint.

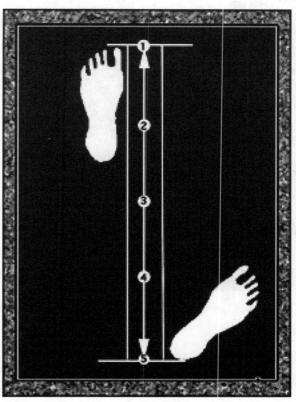

Fig. 4.2 Five points of reference in archer stance

To get into the posture properly, put the knee of the front leg over the bubbling well point of the front foot . Be sure not to extend beyond it. Distribute the weight 50-50 on both feet. Then, first lean the centerline forward to relax the hips while sucking in the abdomen and tucking the pelvis forward and upward. Then, straighten the centerline back to verticality and very carefully straighten the rear leg. *(Fig. 4.3)*

In *wuji qigong* , the emphasis is primarily on `how to cultivate stability and structure around the centerpoint.

Create isometric tension by simultaneously pushing from the front foot into the rear foot and from the rear foot into the front foot. Though externally it may look like 90

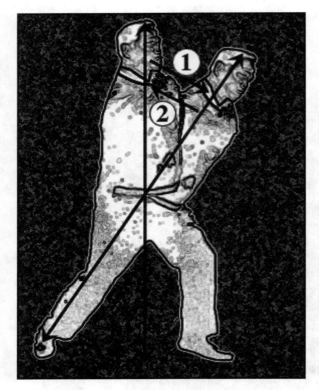

Fig. 4.3 Aligning posture in archer step

percent of the weight is on the front foot, "when the *qi* is right", i.e. the hips are loose, the weight is equalized 50-50, and the centerline is actually aligned along the "three points on a straight line." This is difficult and demanding work. Be aware that straightening the rear leg is to close the knee joint. With your awareness, learn to relax within the closed knee joint. This is the meaning of the phrase "let the joint be open while keeping it closed". When you have this awareness, you will be at the edge of readiness for instantaneous action

In reprogramming the body/mind for use, most of the work in the archer step will be done with the weight distributed 30-70 on front or back. However, for strength training, the weight can be completely on the front or rear foot.

"Let the joint be open while keeping it closed", that is, using your awareness, learn to relax within the closed knee joint

When the weight is 90-100% on the front foot, the knee will be directly above the bubbling well. To do it right, tuck and suck, i.e. tuck the buttocks under, pull in abdomen and fill the lower back. Above all, relax the hips while making these demands. This is the real trick and it is very hard to do.

The isometric tension between the front and rear leg is always maintained, whether the weight (centerline) is on the front or rear foot. Bending the rear leg and sitting on it with most of the weight, the front leg is still bent slightly at the knee. When the hip is truly relaxed, the rear leg will get tired very quickly. Do not sink down too much, for then your structure will be unable to support the centerline and weight. You will not be able to relax the hips and the *qi* will not be able to sink.

The isometric tension between front and rear leg is always maintained, whether the weight (centerline) is on the front or rear foot.

When the weight is on the rear foot, slightly keep the knee either to the inside or to the outside of the bubbling well. It should not be directly above the bubbling well point. This would put too much pressure on the foot. Do not put the weight on the heel; if it is on the heel, it is too far back. However, when the weight is on the front foot, the centerline should be strictly over the bubbling well.

The correct alignment of all the body parts is primary. If you don't have the

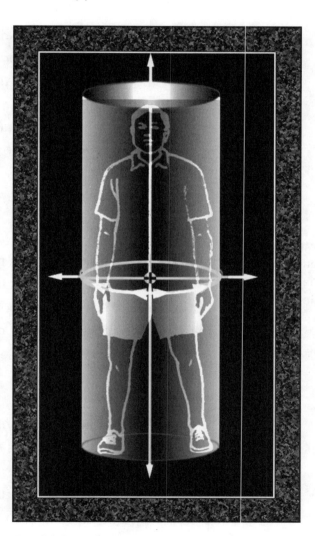

Fig. 4.4 Centerline movements of the human cylinder

71

proper alignment, i.e. if the knee is not over the bubbling well point, if the hips are not even and relaxed, and the *mingmen* is not full in the archer step, you can sit there forever and not feel a thing. All these alignment requirements are not just mechanical rules, but are ways to induce internal feelings/sensations leading to a greater awareness of balance and harmony.

In this connection, it is also supremely important to relax the upper part of the torso. If the chest is tense, you will be unable to turn the waist and rotate the centerline axis properly. Consequently, you will never be integrated, solid. If you pay close attention, you can feel how by relaxing the upper body more pressure is put on the lower part of the body. This makes it more difficult to hold the posture because as the upper body relaxes, the legs will get more sore and tired.

There are three possible centerline movements: up-down, shifting (left-right) and rotation (left-right)

For this reason, it is better to keep a higher stance at first. It will be easier to relax the upper body so the lower body will still be able to support it. Furthermore, the lower you go, the more likely the chance is that one hip will become uneven with the other which must be avoided at all cost.

The mathematics of the polarity principle as it pertains to the centerline determines the number of positions we can hold. There are only three possible centerline movements of the human cylinder: up-down, shifting (left-right) and rotation (left-right) Each type of movement has the three main positions of the two extremes and the middle(center). The up-down movement of the centerline gives three basic height levels: high, center, and low. The shifting movement of the centerline gives three basic weight distribution possibilitites: weight on the left, weight centered between left and right, and weight on the right. The rotational aspect of the centerline gives three

"Foundation building is the real *gongfu* ; all of *gongfu* is based on back and forth, back and forth."

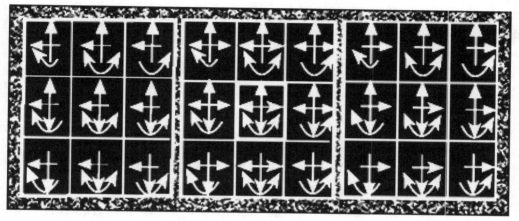

Fig. 4.5 Polarity and the mathematics of centerline positions in parellel stance

basic hip positions: (1) hips square, (2) hips rotated clockwise, (3) hips rotated counterclockwise. When you add it up, this gives 27(3x3x3) basic postures for the parallel stance, as illustrated in the schematic. In the archer step, this is multiplied by two because both the left and right feet can be in front or back. So in archer step you get 54 basic postural permutations plus a literally infinite number of intermediate possibilities.*(Fig. 4.5)*

Shifting

Master Cai said that "foundation building is the 'real *gongfu'*" and "all of *gongfu* is based on back and forth, back and forth. Even I should do more. You can break up a lot of the *taiji* movements into forward and backward parts. Most people don't do it correctly. If you learn the correct way of doing it, you can incorporate it in your *taijiquan* form".

Internally relax the hip with your awareness so the weight/energy can sink down into the rear foot

The range of centerline movement while doing shifting exercises in stationary archerstep is between the second and the fourth points. As you shift forward, stop when your centerline reaches point no.2, and don't go beyond that. Likewise, in shifting back, stop when your centerline reaches point no.4. Beyond these points, you will loose the integrity of your structure, and you will have

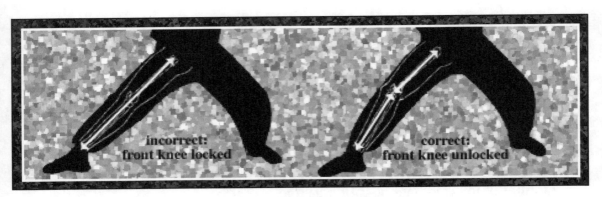

fig.4.6 Front leg alignment

to take a step to reestablish optimum stability. As we will see in pushhands, it is extremely important not to go to the first and fifth points if you don't want to move from your position.

Chapter 4 Being Mindful of the Foundation

How does one know that you've gone too far? In shifting the centerline to the rear foot , if the weight is distributed evenly on the whole foot, you know your centerline is over the fourth point. You stop when the centerline is just over the front/inside of the heel. If it is mostly on the heel, you've gone beyond the fourth point and your structure will be unstable. Now internally relax the hip with your awareness so the weight/energy can sink down into the rear foot. This sinking will distribute the weight/energy evenly all over the foot. Also, be sure that when the centerline is over the fourth point that you keep the front knee unlocked.*(Fig.4.6)* The front leg is not empty; there is still substance pushing against the rear leg in an isometric fashion.

Master Cai heavily emphasized the isometric principle involved in properly shifting the centerline. For example, in shifting from front to rear, he would urge us to push from the front foot while resisting or braking with the rear foot. He likened moving the centerline from the front to rear foot to pushing a boat with an oar or pole from the bottom of the lake or stream. The more you push the front foot (pole) into the ground, the more you (the boat) will move back. The body(centerline), in other words, does not move on its own, but is moved by the pushing of the front (or rear) foot.

Shifting from foot to foot should be done very slowly. You must push from one foot with strength and resist with the other foot with almost but not quite equal strength. Shifting the weight this way is very tiring and creates a

Shifting from foot to foot should be done very slowly; you must push from one foot with strength and resist with the other foot with almost but not quite equal strength.

75

The difficult demand in shifting in Master Cai's way is maintaining the centerline over the middle of the channel.

heavy feeling because you are working with opposing forces to create a compression.

As you push from the front in shifting back, even though you resist with it, you must bend the rear leg a bit so as to be able to sit on it. You cannot keep it straight and locked while trying to shift back; that would immobilize you. When you reach the fourth point, you sink down a little. This sinking is not so much external and physical, but more internal and mental, the purpose being to relax the body with the mind/intention to allow the *qi* energy to sink into the rear foot. At this point it is also very important to relax the upper part of the body, particularly the chest.

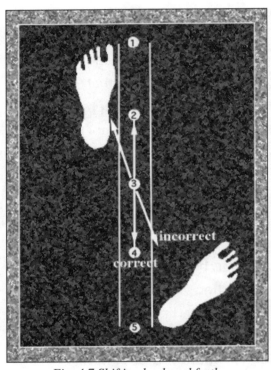

Fig. 4.7 Shifting back and forth

If you are not aware of the relative distribution of tension and relaxation in any and all parts of the body, you are correspondingly "doubleweighted" in those parts.

The most difficult thing in shifting the centerline is to maintain the correct alignment of the "three points on the same line". Even in archer stance, the "earth" point is still the midway point of the line connecting the two bubbling well points. This requires a lot of precision. Here's another way to think of this: When shifting back and forth, the normal tendency is for this shifting to be diagonal in nature. The difficult demand in shifting Master Cai's way is to maintain the centerline over the middle of the channel. *(Fig. 4.7)* The tendency to cross diagonally as one shifts backward or forward is countered by exercising the polarity princicple of opposing forces. The opposing leg/ knee pushes the centerline laterally, keeping it over the channel. This is also why the shifting occurs between the second and the fourth point. Beyond these points, it is impossible to keep the centerline poised above the middle

Just relax the rear knee and make small circles with it—counterclockwise if it's the right knee, clockwise if it's the left knee.

Fig. 4.8 Hand positions during shifting practice

of the channel; it will move diagonally over the foot.

All the principles, demands and awarenesses enumerated for shifting from the front to the rear also apply in shifting from the rear to the front. You push with strength from the rear foot while resisting with the front until the centerline is over the no.2 point and the rear leg is straight though unlocked. Above all, maintain the internal requirements of keeping the centerline plumb, relaxing the hips, and filling the *mingmen* by "tucking and sucking."

At first when shifting, opening and closing, the hands and arms just hang by the side. After practicing this way for a while, then you can put them on the kidneys to help stretch the shoulders. After still more practice, you can raise them in front of the chest in a circle, as if holding the ball/sphere *(Fig. 4.8)*. See also the Chapter 5, "Being Mindful of the Sphere".

A word about double weighting. Generally, this term is used to describe the state of decreased mobility that results when the weight is distributed equally on the two feet. However, it must be stressed that this is true only when talking about the external form and usage without reference to awareness of internal energy. When you have awareness of internal energy, you can shift the energy from leg to leg, i.e., go from empty to full in either leg without external shifting. Thus you can look like you're double-weighted on the outside, but inside you are not. Master Cai calls this ability "double sinking".

Thus double-weighting refers not to any wrong distribution of the weight on the feet but to the lack of awareness of just where the centerline and weight are. More generally, this notion is applicable to the absence of awareness of tension and relaxation in any part of the body. Basically if you are not aware of the relative distribution of tension and relaxation in any and all parts of the body, you are correspondingly "doubleweighted" in those parts.

Rotating (Opening and Closing)

Notice when you shift back by pushing from the front foot that the rear knee will automatically open a bit to make the necessary adjustment in your structure. We take this phenomenon and make a little preparatory exercise out of it for opening and closing the whole body by rotating the centerline. For lack of a better name, we'll call this the "circling-the-knee exercise."

It is really very simple. While in archer stance, keep the hip, the foot and especially the centerline stable and fixed over the third point. Relax the rear knee and make small circles with it—counterclockwise if it's the right knee, clockwise if it's the left knee. *(Fig. 4.9)*

Fig. 4.9 Circling the knee

This turning of the knee is actually not circular, but spherical; it is not two dimensional, but three dimensional. It has not only a horizontal dimension but a vertical dimension as well.

Do this with the weight/centerline on both the front and the rear foot. When on the front foot, bend the rear leg a little, so that the knee can circle. When you're on the rear foot remember to make sure the weight is **not** on the bubbling well but either just on the inside or on the outside of it. When it is centered on the bubbling well, this is like double weighting.

As with all these exercises, program the body by making all movement large initially. First, make large external circles with the knee. Then, for use in martial art, gradually internalize the movement by making the circles smaller and smaller until there is no longer external visible movement, and only the intentional internal movement of energy remains.

Fig. 4.10 Rotating the centerline open

After doing this for a while, you will perceive the fact that this turning of the knee is actually not circular, but spherical; it is not two dimensional, but three dimensional. It has not only a horizontal dimension but a vertical dimension as well. As we shall see, this is the beginning of generating the *sanjijing*, or spiral force, for a spiral is the synthesis of the two opposites of horizontal circular and vertical movement.

There are two basic types of *taiji* energy resulting from the rotational aspect of centerline movement. These are called opening and closing. In developing these two energies in the archer step, the two halves of the body are envisioned as a hinge with the centerline being the hinge pin. One side of the body is kept immobile like the half of the hinge that is screwed into the wall, while the other side can move because it is affixed to the door; one half of the body is like the moving door which opens and closes while the other half is fixed and stable like the wall to which it is attached.

Fig. 4.11 Rotating the centerline in closing

It is important while practicing opening and closing to keep both the hips and the upper part of the body very relaxed. If the top of the body is tense, the exercise will seem easy but in fact the bottom (foundation) will remain unstable. You know you are relaxing the upper part of the torso correctly when the legs begin to feel very heavy and you start having burning and trembling sensations in them.

To practice opening, shift your entire body back so the centerline is plumb over the no. 4 point. *(Fig.4.10)* Then relax the entire body, sinking internally. This sinking assures the greatest stability of the centerline. Then you start the rotation of the centerline with the rear knee simultaneously opening in a half circle. It is also absolutely essential for martial art development to rotate the

The hips and shoulders open together and remain in alignment; the shoulders do not turn any further then the hips and there is no twisting of the spine involved.

*Fig 4.12 Discontinuous circling
in opening and closing*

torso as a unit. That means the hips and shoulders open together and remain in alignment; the shoulders do not turn any further then the hips and there is no twisting of the spine involved.

The essence of this exercise is that when you reach the fourth position, to fix the front leg/knee and not to move it anymore. It is the back leg that opens up. Note though that the front knee will have the tendency to collapse inward, but you must resist this with an opposing intention.

Your intention should be to open as far as possible, even to180 degrees. The arms and hands can help in this. Either (1) stretch both arms sideways or (2) keep the front hand stationary in front of the torso above knee while the shifting hand, carried by the shoulder, reaches out and opens palm up .

If you relax and do it right, i.e. turn with the waist internally, your *qi* will go down and the front leg will feel heavy, solid and tired within one minute; it is normal for it to tremble with fatigue

The exercise to develop and bring out the closing energy is as follows: Fix the centerline on the second point and keep the rear leg straight. Also steady the front knee/leg so it doesn't move at all. Turn the centerline against the front leg as if folding the two sides of the body (especially the hips) onto themselves. *(Fig. 4.11)*Think of the centerline turning 180 degrees. Of course, in actuality you will be limited by your flexibility. The crux is the looseness of the hips. As your hips loosen up, your ability to turn will increase. Like the opening exercise, this is primarily an exercise to increase the flexibility of your hips.

Additional points to remember: Keep the body plumb and keep the lower back straight. At the same time your chest has to remain relaxed and should not be tensed or strained. If you relax and do it right, i.e. turn with the waist internally, your *qi* will go down and the front leg will feel heavy, solid and tired within one minute. It is normal for it to tremble with fatigue under the demand being placed on it. If your chest tenses, your feet will not feel much because the *qi* does not go down at all and you know that this is incorrect. If you stand there and you feel too comfortable, that is actually incorrect. You should feel the *qi* going down the front foot making it unbearably heavy and sore.

The reason you put the hands in the lower back on the kidneys is that it actually helps you to turn the body and centerline. When you reach your limit, your hands can help you go just a little bit further. You may want to force it a little bit by bouncing/pushing the waist over to the side with the hands on the kidneys. That's OK. Once the hips understand the sensation, you can do it without the hands on the kidneys.When you first start combining shifting with the circling of the knee, the tendency will be to make

There is one continuous counterclockwise circle of neutralization and discharge in which the energy flow is never interrupted and always returned smoothly to the point of origin, namely, the opponent.

Fig. 4.13 Continuous circling of the knee in opening and closing

opening and closing opposite half circles. For example, when the right foot is the rear foot, opening is half a circle clockwise; closing is half a circle counterclockwise. This is good for training and stretching of the hips. *(Fig. 4.12)*

However, this is not good for usage since it entails two discontinuous movements. At the end of opening, the movement stops and is retraced in closing. In usage, you want movement to be continuous and circular. Therefore, in later practice make both the half circles of opening and closing go in a counterclockwise direction (still assuming the right leg is the rear). To be more precise, in making the first half circle movement of neutralizing, first move the knee back and then out, and in the second half of circle, the discharging phase, first move the knee forward and then in. This makes for one continuous counterclockwise circle of neutralization and discharge in which the energy flow is never interrupted and always returned smoothly to the point of origin, namely, the opponent. *(Fig. 4.13)*

In practice, you open and close to the maximum degree possible, while in use you open and close only the minimum degree required.

It is appropriate at this time to make some preliminary comments about the relative difference between cultivating opening and closing techniques as described here and their eventual use in martial arts applications. The initial object of practice is to program the body and stretch the ligaments, tendons and muscles; the work is physical. In martial arts, the effort will be almost entirely on the mental and intentional level with as little physical movement as necessary. Therefore, in practice you open and close to the maximum degree possible, while in use you open and close only the minimum degree required. In the martial

84

arts application of opening or closing, you don't attempt to turn 180 degrees, but you will turn only one to two degrees, the slightest movement necessary to do the job, while in the exercises you turn as much as you can.

Some further comments about the opening and closing of joints are appropriate here since these terms apply to all the joints of the body. In general, a joint closes in action and opens in preparation for action. But, and here is the paradox, if a joint opens too much by approaching the limits of its range, it becomes incapable of quick action, especially against the force of an opponent, effectively paralyzing us. Therefore the big movements of opening to extremes are only good for toning the body by stretching the muscles and ligaments.

"Small movement is better than big movement and no movement is better than small movement."

For flexibility, you may want to practice extreme opening of the back by arching back as far as you can at the *mingmen*. This is worse than useless in martial arts, because the upper and lower parts of the torso have become effectively disintegrated. The same is true for the hip joints and all other joints. Hence a maxim of the internal martial arts tradition is that "small movement is better than big movement and no movement is better than small movement". This saying expresses the essence of Master Cai's system, as well as other internal martial arts, such as *yiquan*, that concentrate on the development of intention or *yi*. They teach us the paradoxical ability of keeping the joints mentally or intentionally open while physically closed. By closing the joints, we prevent the dissipation of the *qi*, or energy, and concentrate it inside the joints of the body. Then you have in the physical closing an intentional opening; inside the mechanical locking you have a conscious unlocking; inside the tension you practice relaxation.

We use the looseness of the joints acquired through maximum physical opening and stretching in the closed position. You mentally lengthen and loosen the compression of the joints. By maximizing the space between them, you open them internally. Thus each joint will be integrated-

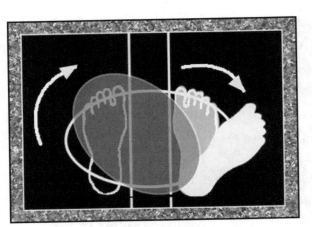

Fig. 4.14 Preparing to step

The stepping exercise "is going from *wuji* to *taiji* because it creates the *yin-yang* polarity of substantial-insubstantial in the foundation."

relaxed, not collapsed-relaxed. This is the ultimate readiness for action. The mere intention of closing of all joints will produce a unified discharge of energy without any external movement.

Stepping And Walking Forward.

Master Cai said that the following stepping exercise "is going from *wuji* to *taiji* because it creates the *yin-yang* of substantial-insubstantial in the foundation." He added that all the other exercises that he taught us before, such as rotating the knee, shifting and rotating the centerline, led up to and are contained within this exercise; they were the foundation for it. "Therefore you need only do this one."

Start out with the feet parallel, with a channel the width of a fist between them. Rotate the centerline 45 degrees, which turns the foot out 45 degrees.*(Fig.4.14)* Sink internally and lower the centerline to the desired level so that it can remain even and not bob up and down while being shifted. Keep the back straight and the *mingmen*

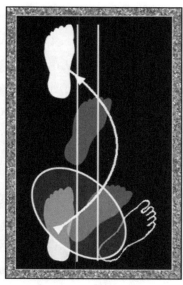

Fig. 4.15 Placing the foot

pushed out. Transfer the center(line) of gravity to the turned out foot. Relax the hip of the weight bearing leg and feel as if the two hips are folding on each other.

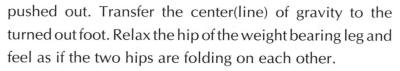

This exercise is another example of the principle of relative motion at work. Only after the foot that has moved is still and stable can the centerline move and be shifted on to it.

Get ready to move the foot by raising the heel of the insubstantial foot so only the toe touches. Then describe a half circle with the empty foot and put it down $2\frac{1}{2}$-3 foot lengths in front of the substantial one, maintaining the width of the channel. First, only practice tracing semicircles back and forth with the insubstantial foot--half a circle forward, half a circle back.*(fig. 4.15)*

Then to add shifting, proceed as follows: After the foot is placed, rotate the centerline back so that the hips are square again relative to the front foot. Then, push-

Fig. 4.16 Stepping & shifting

ing from the rear foot, shift the centerline forward onto the front foot, making the front leg substantial and the rear leg insubstantial. *(Fig. 4.16)* This exercise is another example of the principle of relative motion at work: One leg and centerline are fixed, while the other moves. Only after the foot that has moved is stable can the centerline move and be shifted on to it.

Master Cai repeatedly cautioned us to start this stepping exercise in a high stance and take small steps and work toward lower stances and bigger steps gradually. Initially, if you sink too low, your step will be too long and difficult; your body won't be able to support it, and your structure will be unstable.

Master Cai's *taiji* walking exercise is the next logical

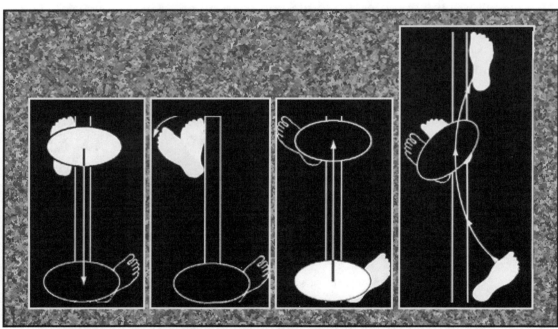

Fig.4.17 Backshifting and turning the front foot out,
shifting and placing the foot in the walking exercise

elaboration on the stepping and shifting exercises. Follow the procedure for stepping and shifting forward as detailed above. Then, when weight is on the front, shift back and rotate the centerline closed simultaneously turning the front foot out 45 degrees. Next, shift forward and pull up the rear leg and place it forward, square the hips and shift the centerline to the front foot.

You are now ready to start the cycle on the other side. Rotate the centerline and close the hips on the front foot. Square and shift back. Open, square, rotate the centerline and front foot out, raise and shift forward. Pull up and step with rear foot, etc. You can see that in walking for practice, an additional shift back is included. *(Fig. 4.17)* Of course, in self-defense or in doing your set you don't have to do that. You can turn the foot immediately by simply shifting the centerline to the heel of the front foot and turning out the toe instead of shifting it back to the rear foot all the way.

At first, in this walking exercise, make your rotating and shifting two separate actions. Later you can combine them into one simultaneous action. In walking, as in all other movements, always keep in mind the two principles that "the outside follows the inside" and "the less you move, the better." In other words, your intention must precede your action and you move as little as you need to in order to maintain your internal integration and comfort.

Regarding the arms in the walking exercise, Master Cai had this to say: "Let the whole body carry your arms. That is, when shifting and rotating, allow the index fingers to follow the centerline movement. This results in harmoni-

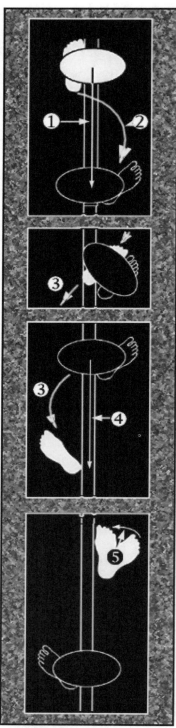

Fig. 4.18 Walking backwards

ous rotations of the lower arms with the centerline .

Stepping And Walking Backward

The practice of stepping and walking backward follows the same general procedure as stepping and walking forward, except in reverse. Start out with the feet parallel, with a channel the width of a fist between them.

Rotate the centerline 45 degrees which turns the foot out 45 degrees. Sink internally and lower the centerline to the desired level so that it can remain even and not bob up and down while being shifted. Keep back straight and the *mingmen* pushed out. Transfer the center(line) of gravity to the turned-out foot. Relax the hip of the weight-bearing leg and feel as if the two hips are folding up on each other.

Get ready to step with the empty foot, say the left foot, by lifting the heel slightly off the ground. As you step back, the left foot will describe a semi circle that first goes to the outside, comes back, and is placed toe out, just on the outside of the central channel. (Note

Chapter 4 Being Mindful of the Foundation

that this is the opposite from the half circle the foot makes in stepping forward where the direction of movement first goes in and then out.) Practice stepping back like this without bobbing the centerline up and down to determine the effective length of your step.

Now you can expand the stepping exercise by stepping forward, backward and sideways, as you wish. The main thing is to keep the centerline steady no matter in which direction you step. Step forward with semicircle first going in, then going out. Retrace this semicircle and place the foot back. Step sideways in a straight line and place the foot back. Step backward in a semicircle, first going out then going back in and retrace this circle when pulling the foot back. Improvise on the order of execution, but always pull the foot back to the center before moving it out in another step.In *taijiquan* walking techniques, most *taiji* teachers just use straight forward and backward steps. Master Cai's basic circular stepping techniques in walking forward and backward give his free walking movement its *bagua (pa kua)* quality.

In shifting backward, first step as described above, and then push from the front foot to shift the centerline to the rear foot. When the weight is on the rear, allow the front foot to turn and adjust so that it faces straight forward.

To walk backward *(Fig. 4.18)*, pick up the front foot, placing it back next to the substantial foot while describing a first-in, then-out semicircle, and then move to the rear position describing a first-out, then-in semicircle. Walking backwards then involves an "s" shaped step when the right foot is moved from front to back and a mirror image "s" when the left foot is moved. These two half circles correspond to the closing and opening of the hips. With the first half circle pulling the front foot next to the rear, the hips are closed; in the second one, putting the foot down backwards, the hips are open.

Other points to remember: Maintain an even height of the centerline; do not let it bob up and down, which means don't make your steps too long. Keep the *mingmen* filled and the upper part of the body relaxed. Also maintain your channel in walking backwards, i.e. do not put the feet down so that they cross.

Chapter 5

Cultivating The Sphere

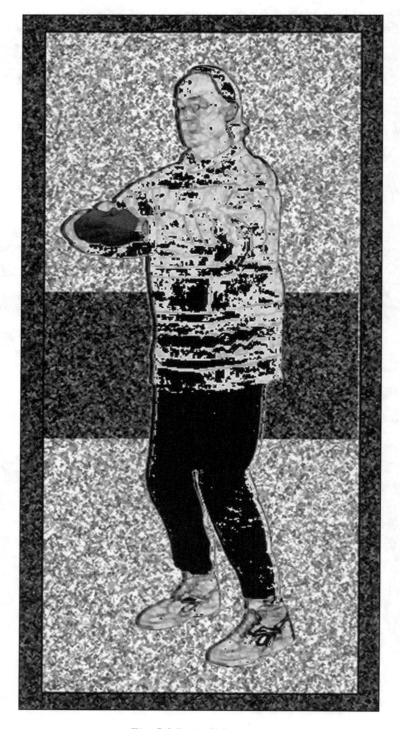

Fig. 5.1 Basic Sphere

Structure and Types of Spheres

Our daily practice with Master Cai always followed the same pattern. First we cultivated the centerline in standing meditation, then we practiced the Centerline movements for building the foundation, and then we practiced the arm movements essential to the making, holding and becoming a sphere.

The basic sphere is made by holding the arms in front of the chest in a circle somewhere between shoulder height and solar plexus height. Any higher will cause the *qi* to rise, any lower will destroy the connection of the circle with the center. The structure of Master Cai's basic sphere is closed, i.e. the hands are touching each other *(Fig. 5.1)*. This is to provide greatest possible integration and integrity of the structure so it will not collapse under pressure from the opponent.

Other salient points regarding its structure are the following: First, relax the shoulders by keeping them low, so that the centerline can carry the sphere. Tense, hunched up shoulders can't distribute the weight of the sphere to the centerline and causes the *qi* to rise, thus disintegrating the sphere and centerline (body).

Second, relax, hollow the chest and round the back to provide a "cushion of space" in front of you. Thus, if you are hit you will not be hurt because there is nothing there. Failure to do this (i.e., if the chest is tense and sticks out with the shoulder blades pulled back) breaks the integrity of the sphere which allows the opponent to control your centerline and strike your body.

Fig. 5.2 Variations of the basic sphere

Third, you must cultivate the intimate connection between the *mingmen* in the lower back and the sphere. Filling the *mingmen*, ie, straightening the lumbar spine by pushing it out to the back activates the sphere. The *mingmen* acts as both trigger and pump which fills the ball with air pressure to discharge energy and repel the opponent.

Filling the *mingmen*, ie, straightening the lumbar spine by pushing it out to the back activates the sphere.

The sphere is more a feeling than a geometric construction. Therefore it can take on an innumerable shapes or manifestations without losing its essential characteristics. Some of the different shapes which are frequently used in Master Cai's system may be defined as: (A) extended, (B) expanded, (C) folded, and (D) half-extended/half-folded. *(Fig. 5.2)*

Further variations on each of these can be obtained by the turning of the forearms and palm. Master Cai's fundamental circle, the universal ward off with both palms facing the body gives rise to the following configurations:

Chapter 5 Being Mindful of the Sphere

(A) and (B) both palms out, (C) press with left palm out and right palm in, (D) crosshands with both palms in; (E) press with right palm out and left palm in, (F). and (G). so called "buddha palm." *(Fig. 5.3)*Vertical Cicrcle

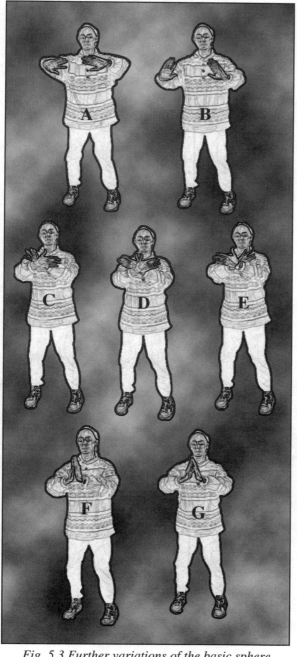

The sphere is more a feeling than a geometric construction. Therefore it can take on innumerable shapes or manifestations without loosing its essential characteristics.

Fig. 5.3 Further variations of the basic sphere

A sphere exists in three dimensions, while a circle exists in only two dimensions. Actually, a sphere may be thought of as an infinity of simultaneous omnidirectional circles around a common center. The sphere our bodies make reflect how we relate to gravity: it consists of two main circles, vertical and horizontal, and an infinite number of possible combinations in diagonal circles. The vertical circle is the most fundamental, then the horizontal, and then the diagonal combinations. *(Fig. 5.4)*

The vertical circle can come in many forms—with both hands at the same time or with hands alternating up and down, one at a time; while standing still, in shifting

Actually a sphere may be thought of as an infinity of simultaneous omnidirectional circles around a common center.

Fig. 5.4 Diagonals of the human sphere

and/or in walking combinations. Always its essence is the same: the path made by the hands and arms in raising and lowering the sphere. As in everything else, in practicing the vertical circle, the important thing is to never just throw your hands up quickly without awareness but to do it slowly, making it a conscious, almost ritual act done with awarenesss of the flow of energy through the body. To raise the sphere, start from the standing position in parallel stance with the hands hanging by the side. Put the awareness in the feet by relaxing the hips and sinking a little deeper by bending the knees a little more. Then, pushing from the feet, trace the path of the energy up the body by mentally enumerating the joints as the energy passes through them: ankle, knee, hip, lower back, middle back (the junction of the lumbar and the thoracic spine), upper back (between the shoulder blades), shoulder, elbows, wrists, and out the hands to some imaginary target outside the body. As the energy rises, the arms begin to raise until the energy reaches and exits the hands.

In practicing the vertical circle, the important thing is to do it slowly, making it a conscious, almost ritual act done with awarenesss of the flow of energy through the body.

Raising the sphere is the first half of the vertical circle. To complete the circle, lower the sphere by retracing the flow of energy backwards through the joints. First you may turn the palms down. This helps focus the intention down to the earth. Then enumerate the joints as the energy sinks down the body: wrists, elbows, shoulder, upper back, middle back, lower back, hips, knees, ankles and feet into the ground. The arms lower gradually as the energy descends down the joints to come to rest by the sides of the body when the energy reaches the soles of the feet and sinks into the ground.

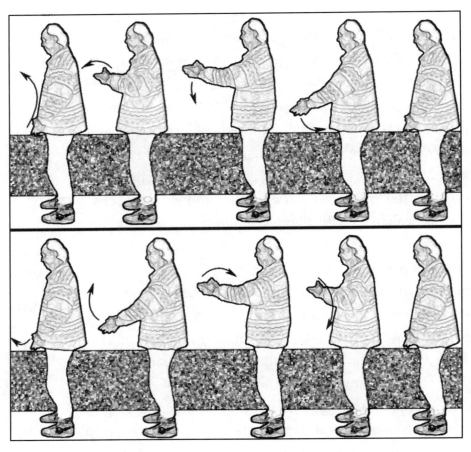

Fig. 5.5 Two ways of practicing the verticle circle

The practice of tracing the energy through the joints in this manner is called "threading the nine pearls". It is an extremely important practice to harmonize the flow of energy through the three springs of the body (legs, torso and arms) and cannot be practiced enough. Its importance is emphasized by the fact that it is also the very first movement of the *Yang* style teaching form.

The practice of tracing the energy through the joints in this manner is called "threading the nine pearls."

The vertical circle can be practiced in two ways *(Fig. 5.5)*. The first way, corresponding to the commencement of the *taiji* form, the direction of the flow of energy is first up and forward, and then back and down. In the second way the direction is reversed. The movement is first up then forward and then down and back . This corresponds to the movement from press to low push to high push in the form.

Again, it's important to emphasize the role played by the *mingmen* in making the vertical circle and threading the nine pearls. Filling the *mingmen* pumps the energy up the back. Failure to do so will leave the upper torso disintegrated from the lower torso and make it impossible to complete the energy cicuit.

Raising and lowering the sphere in the archer step is essentially the same as in parallel stance, except in archer step, there is the added dimension of harmonizing the forward-backward shifting movement of the centerline with the raising and lowering of the sphere. When raising the sphere, start with the weight on the rear foot. While shifting the centerline from the rear to the front foot by pushing from the rear foot and straightening the rear knee and leg, raise the hands making the sphere so that leg, knee and hands reach final position simultaneously.

In practicing the vertical circle, the important thing is to do it slowly, making it a conscious, almost ritual act in which each step is done with awarenesss of the flow of energy through the body.

Vertical circling in the archer step is also an excellent way to demonstrate how the four "main directions" of *peng, an, ji,* and *lu* are derived from the vertical circle. As the path of movement illustrated in *(Fig. 5.6)* shows , the four concepts are energetic in nature and describe the four quadrants of energy of the vertical circle: *peng* as upward (slanting) energy, *ji* as forward energy, *an* as downward energy, and *lu* as backward energy.

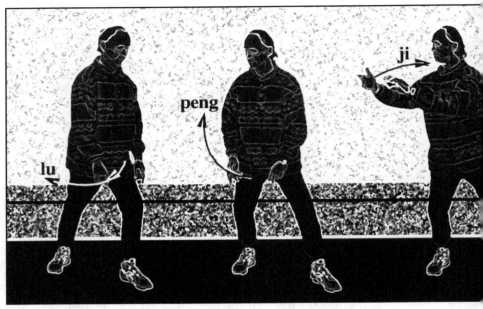

Fig. 5.6 The four main energies derived from the vertical circle

In archer step, there is the added dimension of harmonizing the forward-backward shifting movement of the centerline with the raising and lowering of the sphere.

In the beginning, while threading the nine pearls, it is important to have the actual raising and lowering of the centerline harmonized with the raising and lowering of the sphere. Otherwise it will just degenerate into lifting and lowering the arms without their integration with the rest of the body. Once the path of energy has been thoroughly programmed this way, raising and lowering the sphere (arms) can be done without actual raising and lowering of the centerline and body. This high level of development in which only awareness of the flow of energy is practiced and cultivated is essential for martial arts use.

For developing *li* (strength) as well *yi* (awareness), we take the concept of threading the nine pearls and turn it into an isometric exercise while pushing against a wall. Assume the push posture as illustrated in *(Fig 5.7)* on the

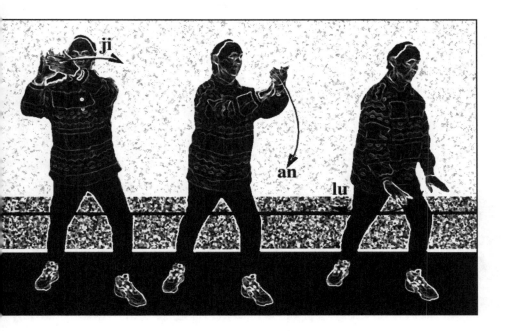

next page. Create an even tension all over the body by pushing your hands against the wall and pushing your feet into the ground. Then "thread the pearls" of the joints by pushing relatively harder from the feet, allowing you to follow the path of the energy flow upward. Count the joints—ankle, knee, hips in the lower spring of the foundation, tailbone, *mingmen* and the point between the shoulder blades in the middle spring of torso, and the shoulders, elbows and wrists in the third spring of the sphere whence the energy exits the body out the palms into the wall. The "foot to palm" direction is the first half of the verticle circle. The reverse "palm to foot" is the second half of the vertical circle. By pushing from the palms into the wall, be aware of the flow of energy backwards from wrist, elbow, shoulder, upper back, middle back, lower back, hip, knee, ankle and from the foot into the ground. Both ways it is important not to lean into the wall while pushing against it or away from it.

Once the path of energy has been thoroughly programmed, raising and lowering the sphere (arms) can be done without actual raising and lowering of the CL and body.

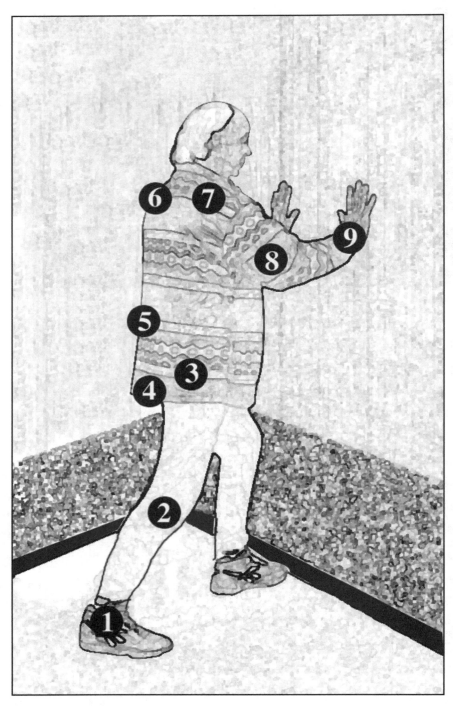

Fig. 5.7 Wooden man/ nine pearls wall pushing exercise

Horizontal Cicrcle

Traditionally, teaching the vertical circle is considered primary, while the horizontal circle is secondary. The vertical circle is considered primary because it embodies the upright cylindrical nature of the human body and entails the body's three springs and nine pearls. The horizontal circle is secondary because it is derived from the rotation of the vertical cylinder around its centerline axis. *(Fig. 5.8)*

Therefore, in the mandalic representation of the eight methods of the thirteen postures, the four corners are considered to be complementary to the four main directions. *Peng, ji, an* and *lu* are represented as the four main directions, because they are derived from the vertical circle. *Kao, zhou, lie,* and *zhai,* are represented as the four corner directions because their functions are derived from the four components of the horizontal circle: the shoulder blade/shoulder, the upper arm/elbow, the forearm/wrist, and the hand, all of which represent the outside periphery of our sphere and which function in conjuction with the rotation of the centerline.

Kao, zhou, lie, and *zhai* are represented as corner directions because their functions are derived from the four components of the horizontal circle: the shoulder blade-shoulder, the upper arm-elbow, the forearm-wrist, and the hand.

Kao, "shoulder stroke," also sometimes translated as "leaning", can be executed either with straight shifting, or with added rotation of the centerline. As the classic says "the skill lies in the shoulders and the back. Spread your hands diagonally. Attack by turning the shoulder, with the back supporting."

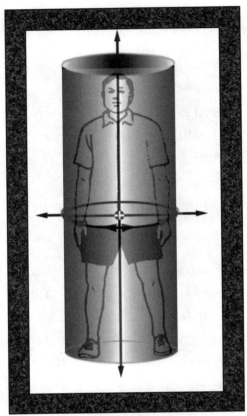

Fig. 5.8 The human cylinder

Practically, "when applying shoulder or elbow stroke, place yourself before the opponent's heel" *(D Wile, p.71)*. The second of the four corners, *Zhou*, "elbow(ing)", like the shoulder, can be done either straight forward with shifting or to the side or back with rotation.

The third of the four corners, *lie*, has many different translations. Huang call it "wristing" , Tam translates it as "twist", and *Yang* Jingming refers to it as "rend" while other writers say "split is in the two forearms" *(D Wile, p.79)*. What they all convey, however, is that the main action of *lie* is with the wrist and the rotation of the forearm in harmony with the rotation of the centerline. What results is two opposing forces applied to the opponent, unbalancing him by rotating him, as expressed in the words of the classic song: "twist strength means...rotate like a flying wheel. Things thrown upon it will rebound yards away."

The classics also counsel that "if we are sealed off by our opponent's ward-off, then we must try *lie* or *zhai*" *(D*

Chapter 5 Being Mindful of the Sphere

Wile, p.71). Zhai is the fourth of the four corners, and variously translated as plucking, picking, pulling or grasping. Whatever the different connotations, all meanings indicate the main action is done with the fingers of the hands confirming the sayings in the classics that *"zhai* is in the fingers" *(D Wile, p.79).* The essence of *zhai* is the subtle use of integrated force to tip the balance scales of equilibrium in our favor. In the words of the classics, *zhai* is "like weights moving on a scale...simply the application of a lever...whatever attack may be imposed, the force can be calculated...adding the weight of a few ounces on the scale, an item of hundred tons can be measured."

Because the horizontal circle is fundamentally a function of the rotational aspect of the centerline, there are two possible horizontal circular energy pathways: clockwise and counterclockwise.

Because the horizontal circle is a function of the rotational aspect of the centerline there are two possible horizontal circular energy pathways: clockwise and counterclockwise, depending on whether the centerline is

Fig. 5.9 Horizontal circle derived from centerline rotation

being rotated to the right or to the left *(Fig. 5.9)*. Because the centerline acts as the center in the horizontal circle, the horizontal circle can go up and down the centerline, by raising or lowering the hands. In other words, the level and plane can change, but not the axis.

In the most basic horizontal circle exercise, have both palms *yin*, i.e facing the body, in a universal ward-off touching each other to complete the circle. See *(Fig 5.9)* In this exercise the circle is strictly connected to, or integrated with, the centerline . Torso and arms turn as a unit. The arms are like the branches on a tree. When the trunk turns, the branches turn. In the martial arts application, the intent is to take the opponent sideways and back, as in the roll-back or *bagua* fish movements.

the centerline acts as the fulcrum of a lever in which your opponent's force exerted on one side of your body may be returned to him by the other side.

In the exercise depicted in *(Fig. 5.10)*, only the torso turns. Unlike the previous exercise, the head and arms do not turn to the side because the mental focus or intent remains straight ahead. Because the hands and arms do not turn sideways with the torso, they are made to move back and forth by the rotation of the centerline*(Fig. 5.10.2a&2b)*. When rotating to the left, the right hand will be pushed forward while the left hand will be pulled back, and vica versa. Think of it as allowing the hips to push/pull the arms and hands.

When we examine the martial arts uses of this variation of the horizontal circle, we will see how the centerline acts as the fulcrum of a lever in which your opponents force exerted on one side of your body may be returned to him by the other side.

Fig. 5.10 Circling with open sphere

Diagonal Circling

Combining the vertical and horizontal circles, we obtain an infinite number of diagonal circles along the surface of our sphere. The exercises depicted in *(Fig. 5.11)* program the body to make diagonal circles, giving us a complete range of spherical movement. Holding a ball in the horizontal circle *(Fig. 5.11.1)*, imagine a rod from the palms to the centerline. This imaginary rod is the axis along which the up and down movement of the elbows will make the basic diagonal circle. As one elbow goes up, the other goes down.*(Fig. 11.5.2a&2b)* Note that the shoulders act as pivots, but do not themselves go up and down.. Keep them relaxed and low. Again, you can change the plane, i.e. have the hand high or low, but you cannot change the axis.

Fig. 5.11 Diagonal circling with closed sphere

The next exercise adds another level of freedom and complication by allowing the turning of the forearms and palms. Keeping awareness of the axis from palms to centerline, as the elbows go up and down, experiment and play by alternately putting the left and right palm in front by circling them around each other and turning the forearms and palms to create even more spherical structures and movements *(Fig. 11.5.3a&3b).*

Lastly, add the rotation of the centerline itself to create an infinite number of possible spherical figure 8 type movements while maintaining the basic structure intact*(Fig. 11.5.4a&4b).*

Circling With Folding-Extending

The exercise illustrated in *(Fig 5.12)*, is extremely important in preprogramming the body for classical pushhands as well as for developing the frame. In the words of Master Cai: "It is the main practice".

Start from the fundamental compacted sphere or balloon so where the *laogong (lao kung)* point of the left palm rests on the crease above the right elbow*(Fig 5.12A)*. Keep in mind that while the outside appearance of this compacted sphere and its extended variations may appear square, that internally it should continue to feel round and spherical.

Using the elbow as pivot, reach forward and out with the right hand, extending the sphere. Keep the palm *yin,*

Keep in mind the necessity to harmonize the upper and lower parts of the torso. The chest and shoulders must be relaxed; the hips must be relaxed before the shoulders and chest can be relaxed.

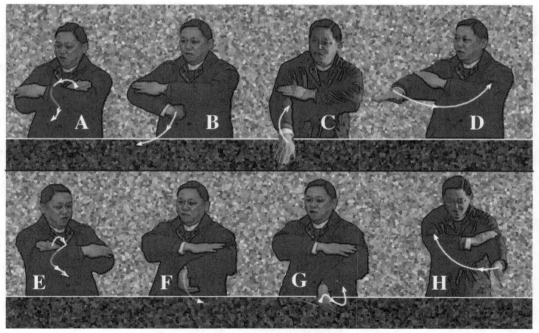

Fig. 5.12   Circling with folding-extending

i.e. facing down.The extended arm is internally relaxed, i.e. straight but not locked(Fig 5.12B-D).

Using the elbow as the pivot, pull the right arm back to the the body and place it on top of the left uppper arm, again with *laogong* point just above the crease of the left elbow(Fig 5.12E).

Change the left palm by curling it towards the body, fingers touching the chest at the point of the centerline (Fig 5.12F), circling it down under the right forearm and then extending it forward and out, again using the (left) elbow as pivot and keeping the palm down(Fig 5.12)G-H. The curling of the forearm is to provide greater integration of the sphere and prevent its collapse under the eventual pressure of the opponents force pushing on it

Visualize taking the *qi* energy from the centerline and extending it with the *yi* or intention down the arm. When the energy reaches the wrist straighten it and project the energy out the hand towards some target in the distance.

In the stage of *yi* or intention training, all movement is gradually internalized, i.e. made smaller and smaller until externally there is no more visible movement; internally, however, there is plenty of activity.

To start cycling through the exercise, repeat the procedure on the other side alternately extending and withdrawing the forearms. Bring the left hand back and put it on the right upper arm. Curl the right hand to the center and extend it, etc. Throughout, keep in mind the necessity to harmonize upper and lower parts of the torso. The chest and shoulders must be relaxed; the hips must be relaxed before the shoulders and chest can be relaxed.

Chapter 5 Being Mindful of the Sphere

Stages Of Practice

Master Cai's instructions on the advanced practice of movement, whether of foundation work, circling exercises, combination thereof, or the entire set of teaching , is entirely in accord with those set forth in the classics. In the first stage, when learning the mechanics of the movement, the stances, steps and circles are of medium size to habituate the body and to avoid making excessive demands on it. In the second stage, stances are lower, steps are longer and deeper and the circling movement of the sphere are larger. In this stage greater demands are made on the body structure to stretch, loosen and strengthen it. In the third stage, in accord with the saying that "small movement is better than big movement, and no movement is better than small movement", *taiji* returns to *wuji*.

This is the stage of *yi* or intention training. All movement is gradually internalized, i.e. made smaller and smaller until externally there is no longer any visible movement; internally, however, there is plenty of activity. The *yi* or intention is directing the *qi* (energy) to produce the sensation of whatever movement is desired. For example, in opening and closing, gradually make the movements of opening and closing smaller until at last you have no physical movement, but you have the physical sensation of opening and closing produced by the mere intention of opening and closing.

As another example, try this with the "threading the nine pearls" vertical circle exercise. Do the exercise for a few minutes with medium size circles as described at the beginning of this chapter. Then, everytime you thread the pearls, make a smaller circle with the arms until eventually there is no more visible external movement, but internally you continue threading the pearls and have the sensation of circling the arms. This is intentional movement in which the focus of awareness is no longer of the energy of movement but on the movement of energy.

One purpose of master Cai's emphasis on stillness over movement is to develop stillness in movement. In normal everyday movement, we can only experience the outward energy of movement. Practicing stillness, we learn to cultivate the experience of the inward movement of energy. Once we have learned this, the internal movement of our energy will inform and direct the external movement of our bodies.

Chapter 6

Combining Centerline, Foundation And Sphere

Threading The Nine Pearls, Continued

The four main *taiji* concepts of *peng, an, lu,* and *ji* are generally translated, respectively, as ward-off, push, roll back and press. These common English renderings have contributed significantly to misunderstanding of these terms by encouraging people to think of them as postures.

In fact, it must be stressed that *peng, an, lu,* and *ji* represent far more than mere postures; they are basic *taiji* **energies** that can be used in any *taiji* posture. Ultimately, indeed, they represent the energetic polarities that are the expression of the vertical circle of the human sphere. *Peng* (ward off) and *an* (push) represent the up and down energetic polarity of the vertical circle. *Peng* is an upward rising/lifting energy, while *an* is a downward pushing/pulling energy. *Lu* (roll back) and *ji* (press) are the backward-forward energetic polarity of the vertical circle. *Lu* is drawing, pulling, absorbing energy backward, while *ji* is projecting energy forward.

Peng, an, lu, and *ji* represent far more than mere postures; they are basic *taiji* energies **that can be used in any *taiji* posture.**

With this in mind, let us revisit the "threading the nine pearls" exercise discussed in the previous chapter. First of all, "threading the nine pearls" goes beyond being a specific exercise; it is a concept of practice in search of an energetic experience, applicable to all *quan* (martial arts). In the following exercise, Master Cai taught us how the concept of 'threading the nine pearls" is combined with the four energies *peng, an, lu,* and *ji* of the vertical circle.*(Fig. 6.1)*

1. *Peng*—upward energy. Get into archer step with left foot forward with arms hanging by the sides and sit on the rear, right foot. Rotate the centerline to open; simultaneously, the forearms also rotate, holding a low ball. Begin to rotate the hips square, push up by straightening the knee and push forward from the foot, simultaneously raising the sphere and putting the right palm on the left wrist .

All these four actions should be harmonized and reach their final point of destination simultaneously, the weight on the front foot, the hips square, and the sphere high. In the process, say to yourself silently the three joints of each

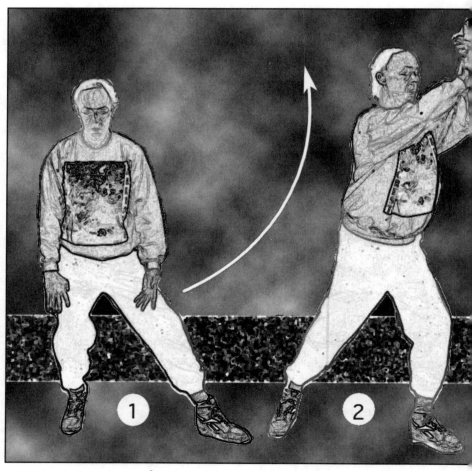

four energies exercise

of the three body springs as the energy moves through them: ankle, knee, hip in the spring of the foundation, lower back, middle back, upper back in the torso spring, shoulder, elbow, wrist in the spring of the sphere. Specifically, don't begin to move the arms until the energy reaches the neck. Also notice that the middle finger is pointing up indicating the projecting of the energy out the hand and up.

   2.*An*—downward energy. Now, keeping weight on the front foot, sink the centerline while separating the hands and pushing (or pulling) down with them until the

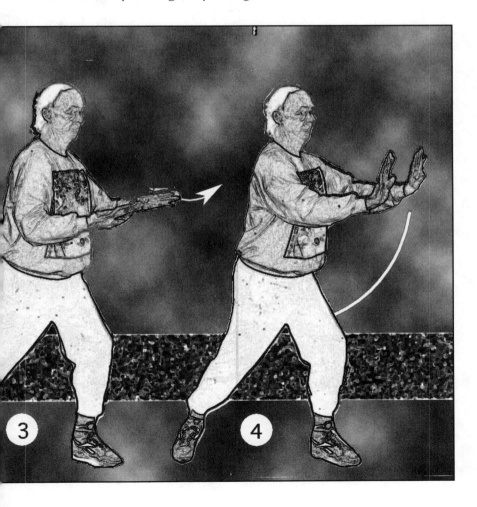

height of the chest or stomach level. In this process, the energy reverses course and travels the nine pearls downward in the opposite direction. Again, enumerate the joints as the energy moves through them: wrist, elbows, shoulders, upper back, middle back, lower back, hips, knees, ankles, from the soles into the ground to the center of the earth.

3. *Ji*—forward, projecting energy. Again reverse the direction of the energy: ankle, knees, hips, lower back, middle back, upper back, shoulders, elbows, wrists and forward out the hands. Notice that this is almost entirely an internal process with very little external movement. The weight remains on the front foot; there is no raising of the centerline and the forward expansion of the sphere (arms and hands) is entirely triggered and controlled by the backward filling and expansion of the *mingmen* .

> "Grasping the Bird's Tail" is a symbolic term in which the bird's tail represents the arm of the opponent, the movement of which is followed as it goes up and down, and rotating to the right or left in order to control it.

4. *Lu*—backward, absorbing energy. The flow of energy again reverses. While pushing from the front foot to shift the centerline to the rear foot, sinking and rotating open, lower the sphere and rotate the forearms. While doing this, again enumerate the joints as the energy passes through them: wrists, elbows, shoulders, upper back, middle back, lower back, hips, knees, ankles, down to the center of the earth. This returns us to the starting position to begin the cycle again.

**

Grasping The Birds Tail Sequence

Almost all published accounts agree that the postures *peng*, *an*, *lu*, and *ji* (ward off, roll back, press and push) are the classical foundation of teaching martial arts training. Demonstrated in *(Fig. 6.2)* by Yang Chengfu, the creator

Yang Cheng Fu's Grapsing The Bird's Tail

of modern Yang style teaching form, they have been collectively known as *lanquewei (lan ch'ueh wei)* or "Grasping the Bird's Tail." This is a symbolic term in which the bird's tail represents the arm of the opponent, the movement of which is followed as it goes up and down, rotating to the left or to the right to control it.

However, while the postures may be agreed upon, there is no such agreement on the movements linking these postures. With each author/practitioner adding his own insights and embellishments, a bewildering number of interpretations has resulted, each differing in detail from the others.

Fig. 6.3. Yang Style Grasping The Bird's Tail

As my starting point I'll use the description provided by Yang Chengfu's youngest son Yang Zhenduo (Yang Chen Tuo) in his book *Yang Style Taijiquan.* This description agrees with what I learned from Master Ha, a student of Yang Shouzhong, the oldest son of Yang Chengfu. Thus, we can be reasonably sure of approximating the original sequence as practiced by Yang Cheng Fu. Following the standardized Yang style set formulated by the Chinese government, I take the liberty of doing both single and double ward off on the same side. *(Fig. 6.3)* This allows the

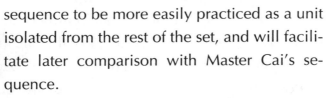

sequence to be more easily practiced as a unit isolated from the rest of the set, and will facilitate later comparison with Master Cai's sequence.

1. Start in left archer step with the weight 70 percent on the front and 30 percent on the back. Raise the left palm in front of the chest and facing it in single *peng*; counterbalancing the left hand, press the right hand down by the right thigh.

2. Shift backward, rotate the centerline to open the hips and begin to circle the left hand upward.

3. Rotate the centerline to square the hips, shift forward and continue to circle the left hand until it is behind the left hand in double *peng*. The hands are as if holding a volleyball.

4. As the weight and centerline stay on the front, rotate the centerline closed to turn the torso 45 degrees to the left. As the centerline rotates, rotate the forearms so that the left palm is *yang*, i.e. facing out, and the right palm is *yin*, i.e. facing the body. Note that the hands do not reverse position. Although the forearms rotate, the left hand stays in front of the right arm.

5. Shift the centerline to the right rear foot until the is weight is 70 percent on the rear, 30 percent on the front. As you shift, drop the hands and rotate the forearms so that the right palm faces down and the left palm faces up, being careful to keep them aligned with the vertical plane of the shoulders.

6. Sitting on the rear foot, rotate the centerline open 45 degrees to the left As you do so, make a half circle with the right hand until it is shoulder height in front of the right shoulder. This intermediate posture, like the one in no.3, is really a right ward off facing sideways to the back.

7. Rotate the centerline to where the hips are square to the front and shift the weight back to the front, left foot. As you do so, bring the left hand in front of your chest. Continue the circling motion with your right hand until it comes to rest with the palm on the left wrist in the press posture.

8. Separate the hands so that each is in front of their respective shoulder with the palms facing down. Shift the weight back to the rear foot, lowering the hands as if pushing or pulling something down.

9. Again, shift the weight to the front foot with the hands circling up and pushing forward.

Master Cai's Grasping The Bird's Tail

All of these elements of centerline movement are built into "grasping the bird's tail," the *taijiquan* sequence comprising the postures "ward-off," "roll-back," "press" and "push." "Grasping the bird's tail," as mentioned earlier, is really the essence of *taijiquan* as a martial art, because it's the basis of all push-hands or double exercises.

Chapter 6 Combining Centerline, Foun dation and Sphere

Master Cai's own version of Grasping The Bird's Tail evolved through many years. The version presented here is based on a series of photographs I took while on a retreat with him at Lake Tahoe in 1986. Here's how to coordinate the arm and hand movements with the movement of the centerline in Master Cai's version of Grasping The Bird's Tail *(Fig. 6.4)*

1. In archer stance with left foot forward and the arms hanging at the sides, shift the centerline back, sink, and rotate the centerline to open the pelvis.

2,3. Next, as your centerline rotates square, rises and shifts forward, your right hand circles up until it touches and presses on the rising left hand in a forward direction.

4,5. As your centerline closes, your forearms rotate, the right palm facing away from the body, the left toward it.

6. As your centerline shifts back, both arms drop by the side of the body.

7,8. As your centerline sinks and opens, your right hand rises in front of the right shoulder.

9,10. As the centerline closes, rises and shifts forward, your left hand comes up in front of the center of the chest and your right hand closes in to press on the left wrist .

11,12. Your left forearm folds under your right forearm.

13. Your left hand and forearm point forward, while the right hand remains resting on the left arm above the elbow.arm.

14. Your centerline shifts back and opens, your right hand separates from the left arm in the roll-back.

15-17. With your weight remaining on the rear foot, square your centerline and sink with the hands pushing down in a low push.

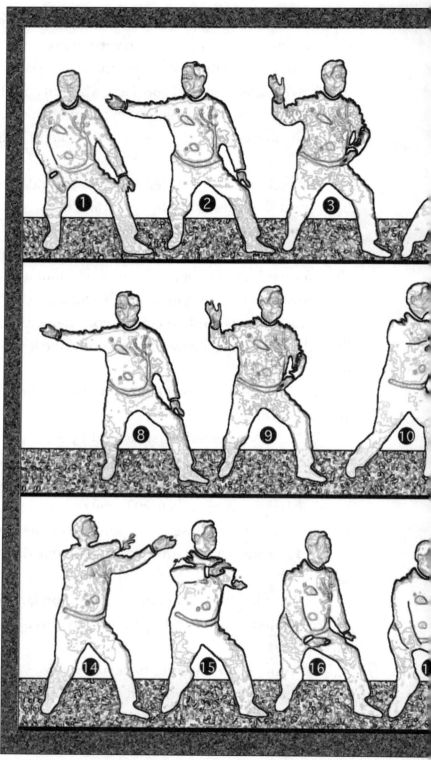

Fig. 6.4. Master Cai's Grasping The Biord's Tail

18, 19. As your centerline rises and shifts forward, the hands/arms rise in a high push.

20. Drop your hands and repeat the sequence.

Practice each sequence as often as possible in both the left and right archer stances.

In Master Cai's version of GBT, there are at least four different kind of presses: on the hand, on the forearm, and on the upper arm. The concept is indeed that the press can be used all along the arm where appropriate to defend against push or pull. But, more importantly, it represents Master Cai's preference that the circle or sphere be closed rather than open with the hands separated.

Spiral Energy Force

The "Threading the Nine Pearls" concept and the Grasping The Bird's tail sequence also manifest a very important concept in the teaching tradition, namely the concept of *chansijin (ch'an ssu chin)*, or "spiral force." In nature, a spiral happens when the polarity of circular and linear forces occur simultaneously. The human *chansijin* is an example of the vertical spiral, in which horizontal circular movement is combined with vertical linear movement.

The horizontal circular energy is generated by the circling of the knee along with the rotation of the centerline and the turning of the forearms, while the vertical energy is simultaneously generated by the upward pushing from the foot and the raising of the centerline. Thus the three

Thus the three springs of the human body are integrated by horizontal and vertical circular movement to produce a spiral energy.

128

springs of the human body are integrated by horizontal and vertical circular movement to produce a spiral energy.

Master Cai's teaching and practice of the *chansijin* seems at variance in some important ways with the teachings presented by most instructors and as described in most printed texts. The main difference is that generally the *chansijin* is said to originate in the bubbling well, while Master Cai generates it by the circling of the knee while the foot and hip are kept stable. He says if you try to start it in the foot, you will not be able to get up beyond the knee.

When you have learned to internalize both the vertical and horizontal energy components of the spiral, you will have refined your external spiral movements of *chansijin* into *chousijin (ch'ou ssu chin)* or "reeling silk" energy, which is the intentional spiral of purely internal energy.

According to Master Cai's conception, the knee is the middle point of the spring or lever of the leg, the foot and the hip being the lower and upper points, and the circling of the knee will activate or carry both the the lower and upper points, the foot and the hip. This is analogous to the splitting of the centerline energy at the *wuji* center point with half of it sinking down into the root and half of it rising to the head as discussed in Chapter 2.

Actually, when we take into account the vertical and horizontal dimensions of the spiral force, we can agree with the traditionalist that the *chansijin* energy starts from the bubbling well point in the foot because the vertical upward energy is generated from that point by the foot pushing down into the ground. Master Cai is also right because the horizontal dimension of energy is first generated by the circling (opening and closing) of the knee.

When you have learned to internalize both the vertical and horizontal energy components of the spiral, i.e the raising of the centerline by pushing from the feet, the rotations of the knee, centerline, and forearms (palms), you will have refined your external spiral movements of *chansijin* into *chousijin (ch'ou ssu chin)* or "reeling silk"

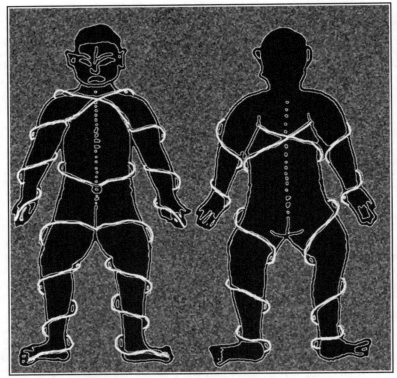

Production of human spiral force or chansijin

energy, which is the intentional spiral of purely internal energy. *(Fig. 6.5)*

As we have seen in the "threading the nine pearls" in the "pushing the wall" exercise, there are two routes the energy can travel through the nine joints of the body which together constitute the vertical circle. In discharging energy, integral force begins in the foot, travels up the leg and back, and then down the arms and is discharged out of the hand. In neutralizing an opponent's energy, it follows the reverse path: it is received by and travels up the arms, down the back and legs to be absorbed in the earth through the feet.

This means that there are also two basic types of spiral energy. In the discussion of spiral energy, we have ana-lyzed its generation in the leg, its propulsion up the back and its expression or discharge from the arms(hands). Obviously, the reverse route of the neutralizing energy pathway constitutes a mirror image reverse spiral. The Chen school calls the former *shun chansijin* (normal spiralling) and equates it with *peng jin (p'eng chin)* or ward-off energy , and calls the latter *ni chansijin* (reverse spiraling) and equates it with *lu jin* or pull and roll-back energy. See *Taiji Magazine*, April 1991, p.15.

Pure *Yin* and *Yang* Exercises

Master Cai's has never practiced, nor even learned, the classical form of *taijiquan.* For some 30 years, the sequence of Grasping the Bird's Tail was the only se-quence of movement he practiced because he feels that Grasping The Bird's Tail contains the essence of *taijiquan* as a martial art and that the practice of forms detracts from the practice of essence. If your aim is to look pretty, by all means practice forms; if your aim is to develop martial art to your highest possible level, don't bother with forms. Practice only standing and Grasping The Bird's Tail.

pure yin exercise

In the 1980s, however, Master Cai gradually stopped his practice of Grasping The Bird's Tail in favor of two movement sequences which he calls the "pure *yin* " and "pure *yang* " exercises. Although very short, the "pure *yin* " and "pure *yang*" exercises are very subtle and hard to describe verbally because the external movement is only the expression of the intentional and energetic processes going on internally.

The description and analysis presented here of the "pure *yin* " and "pure *yang*" exercise will be flawed and incomplete. While Master Cai, at our request, demonstrated them numerous times, he has not (yet) provided us with detailed explanations as to the flow of energy and the use of intention in each and every little movement. However, I will attempt to share here my own practice of them combined with the hints that Master Cai did give.

"Pure *Yin*" Exercise

1. Start in *wuji* stance, feet parallel shoulder-width apart and hands hanging by the sides.

2. Using the principle of "threading the nine pearls, let the energy start from the feet, travel up the legs and torso and lift the arms, in a circulatory expanding manner until they hold the sphere in front of the chest. This is upward rising energy or *peng* .

3. Draw the hands back closer to the chest in a half circle, absorbing the energy into the centerline. This is *lu*, backward absorbing energy.

4. Expand the hands horizontally forward in a semicircular manner. This is *ji*, forward expanding energy.

5. Lower the hands to waist level palms down, keeping the elbows steady and turning the forearms so that the fingers of the hands point toward each other. This is *an*, or downward sinking energy.

Pure Yang exercise

6. Again using *peng*, upward raising energy, raise the energy up the back, the hands also rising along with the energy.

7. Again using *an*, downward sinking energy, sink the energy and hands down the front of the body.

8. In conclusion,open the shoulders and rotate the arms, positioning the hands next to the side of the body..

This subtle movement is actually *lu*, or aborbing energy. Finally, lower the hands back iinto *wuji* posture.

The "Pure *Yang*"

The "pure *yang*" exercise is an elaboration of the "pure *yin* " exercise. A few additional movements are added to the pure *yin* sequence.

1-6. Do the "pure *yin*" until the point where the energy rises up the back and the hands are in front of the chest, fingers pointing to each other.

7. Using *ji*, forward expanding energy, turn the palms out and expand arms forward in a circular manner.

8. Simultaneously, sink the entire body into a very low stance, lower the arms to waist level with the backs of the hands touching each other. This is using *an*, downward sinking energy.

9-11. Using *peng*, upward rising energy, raise the centerline and the arms until they are chest level. Then separate the hands so they are in front of their respective shoulders.

12. Using *ji*, forward expanding energy, push the hands forward with the shoulders and back simulta- neously expanding backwards.

13. Using *an*, downward sinking energy, lower the arms to waist level.

14. To conclude, again turn the arms to position the hands next to the side of the body and lower them into the *wuji* stance.

Master Cai always emphasizes the "pure *yin*" exercise as more basic than the "pure *yang*," and keep in mind that the "pure *yang*" consists of "pure *yin*" plus some additional movements. When analyzed, the "pure *yin*" exercise seems to consist of two vertical and one horizontal circle, while the "pure *yang*" has two additional horizontal and one additional vertical circle.

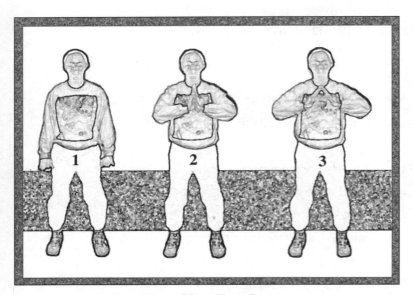

Pure Yin and Pure Yang Postures

Master Cai has not spoken about the origins of the pure *yin* and *yang* exercises. However, a tantalizing clue is provided by Fang Naili in his book *WUJISHI Breathing Exercise* where he presents Master Cai's "pure *yin*" and "pure *yang*" **postures** as auxiliary meditation postures to basic *wuji* posture. Thus, as with the Grasping the Bird's tail sequence, the moving excercises of "pure *yin*" and "pure *yang*" are derivative from still postures.

The main difference with Grasping the Bird's Tail is that the "pure *yin*" and *"*pure *yang*" exercises are done in parallel stance, while Grasping the Bird's Tail is always done in the archer step. Besides the obvious fact that you don't have to change legs in order to exercise both halves of the body equally, the main effect of the parallel stance is in the nature of the centerline rotation and the horizontal circle. In the archer step of Grasping the Bird's Tail, the centerline of the body is rotated right and left separately to alternately produce clockwise and counterclockwise horizontal circles. In parallel stance, the clockwise and counterclockwise circles are actually made simultaneously, cancelling each other out externally but not energetically. What results is a postural condition which is like the embodiment of a standing wave. A potential is contained in stillness, ready at the slightest intention for kinetic expression.

> In parallel stance, the clockwise and counterclockwise circles are made simultaneously, cancelling each other out externally but not energetically. What results is a postural condition which is like the embodiment of a standing wave.

This analysis is substantiated in an early version of the "pure *yin*" exercise in which Master Cai alternately rotated left and right, so that the energy traveled from the left hand up the left arm and down the right arm into the right hand in a counterclockwise horizontal circle and vice versa in a clockwise horizontal cirChapter 6

PART III

BEING MINDFUL OF THE CONNECTION

HOW TO USE AWARNESS OF
RELAXATION AND INTEGRATION IN MARTIAL ARTS

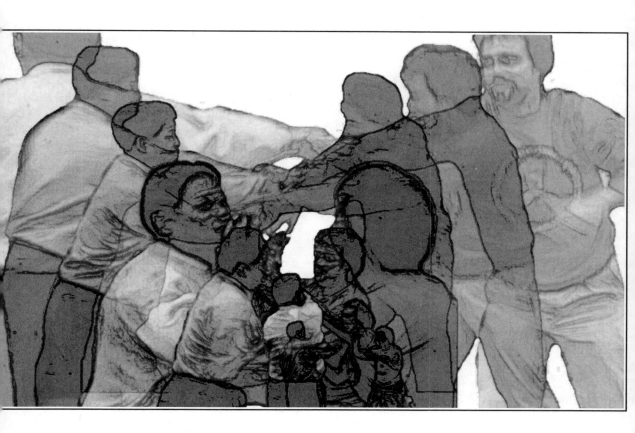

Chapter 7

Using Energy and Strength

In Partnered Practice

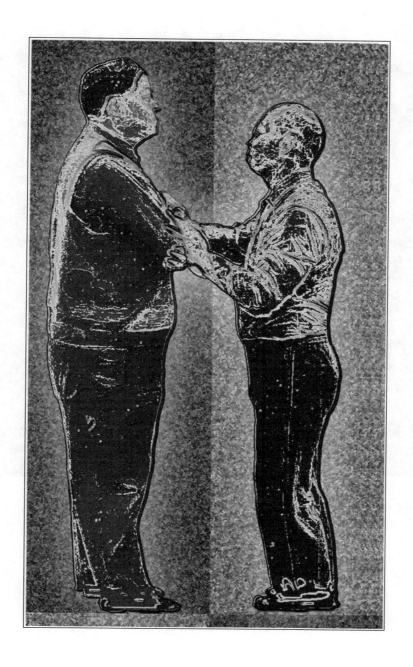

Fig. 7.1 The human sphere is defined by the centerline

The Sphere of *Peng*

The lessons in this chapter teach us how to cultivate our awareness of the flow of energy while our body-mind is interacting with a partner/opponent. In stillness, we discover how to use the structure of our human sphere and learn how to control it with awareness.

As our basic structure, our upright posture gives us a vertical cylinder on a bipedal base. The human sphere is first and foremost defined by the vertical dimension of the centerline *(Fig. 7.1)*. This makes the vertical circle the primary dimension of the human sphere. One-half of the vertical circle is *yang*. This is the path of discharging energy which starts in the feet and goes up the body and is expressed in the hands. The opposite half of the vertical circle is *yin* in nature. It is the path of neutralizing (the opponent's) energy and goes from hands down the body into the feet.

We need to learn how to cultivate awareness of the flow of energy while our body-minds are interacting with those of our partners/ opponents'.

The second defining element of the human sphere is the energy of the horizontal circle, which is created by the rotational aspect of the vertical centerline. The horizontal circle embodies the old saying that "to neutralize is to attack." We will investigate and practice the combination of vertical and horizontal energy circles into (1) diagonal circles, and (2) the creation of spiral energy.

The Chinese term for the feeling of human sphericity is *peng*. The five elements of central equilibrium, shifting forward and backward, and gazing (rotating) left and right, all refer to the centerline and its possible movements on the foundation. *Peng* is the the most important of the eight basic methods or techniques which involve the arms and the sphere. *Peng* is usually translated as ward-off, but this translation does not do justice to the true scope of its meaning. Its true sense is better grasped just from the sound of *peng* like something bouncing off something else.

"*Taijiquan* is *pengquan (p'eng ch'uan),*" Master Cai would often repeat in this connection while discussing the nature of the sphere. It is important to realize that the *taiji* concept of the human sphere refered to by Master Cai entails far more than just the ball held by the arms. Indeed, it embraces the entire human body, literally from toes to fingertips with the *wuji* point as the center. As such *peng* is far more than a single posture or technique; it refers to an awareness of integration which must be a part of every *taiji* posture and movement.

The true sense of *peng* is better grasped just from the sound of *peng* like something bouncing off something else.

In one of the few intelligent discussions on the subject available in English, Mike Sigman presents a good analysis of *peng*, in an article entitled "Qi and Internal Strength" (*QI Magazine*, V1, #1, Spring 1991). Sigman's treatment is in accord with Master Cai's teachings on the subject and identifies the two defining characteristics of *peng* as "aligned strength" and "connection".

What Sigman means by aligned strength of *peng* is the use of "non-rigid skeletal muscle to propagate loadbearing to the ground" He gives as an example people carrying large loads on their heads for long times without the use of prohibitively large energy expenditures. This is the essence of Master Cai's main practice of *wuji* centerline meditation which aligns our posture and cultivates our awareness.

Secondly, what Sigman calls "connection", Master Cai calls "integration", and refers to what the classics call "threading the nine pearls", i.e."a relaxed, barely percep- tible tensile connection from the feet, through the body and the back, to the arms." Without integration, you won't be able to move the arms and hands with the center(line); you will be forced to rely strictly on the use of local muscle.

Without integration, you won't be able to move the arms and hands with the centerline; you will be forced to rely strictly on the use of local muscle.

Master Cai calls his approach to the cultivation of *peng*, "wooden man" training. "Wooden man" is a more poetic expression for what we will also call the "frame", and can be best defined as the polar opposite of the concept of "posture". If a posture, in the *taiji* sense, refers to a particular bodily configuration in space which is held with a maximum of awareness and relaxation (*song*), a frame is the same spatial configuration maintained with tensile strength. Thus, at the extreme poles of this polarity a posture is *yin* (or insubstantial), while a frame is *yang* (or substantial). Otherwise put, a frame is a posture with tension and a posture is a frame without tension.

This polarity represents a spectrum, and our bodily configurations will be usually somewhere along the spec- trum, a mixture of *yin* and *yang*, depending on the needs of the moment. In fact, the true art of *taijiquan* lies precisely in perceiving what mix of posture and frame (*yin* and *yang*) is appropriate for any given defensive or offensive need and the ability to instantaneously go from one to the other in the proportion required.

Receiving a force is always done with *peng*, the principle and technique that senses and interprets the nature and strength of the incoming force and distributes it evenly throughout the body, so that no one local part, including the points of contact, is exerted more than any other. Wherever an opponent touches, he will constantly encounter what is described as a soft "pressure" which increases the harder he pushes."

Peng senses and interprets the nature and strength of the incoming force and evens it out throughtout the body, so that no one local part, including the points of contact, is exerted more than any other.

To ready your *peng* and get in the proper frame of body and mind to neutralize a force, you must first be still and expand your *mingmen* backwards, then feel the *qi* in the shoulders and follow it with the eyes until it reaches the elbows. Then the pressure inside and outside will be the same, and you can move your sphere and/or centerline as much, or rather as little, as necessary. Never worry about the person pushing on you and above all never tense up when you are pushed. You need only to think about your *mingmen* and expand it to inflate your *peng* and even out your opponent's force throughout your body.

It is very important to learn the distinction between tension that resists and the apparent solidity of the *peng* frame which welcomes and accepts energy while neutralizing it. The distinction is based on control. If you are doing the pushing, when you meet resistance you will be able to control your opponent's centerline and push him, but when you meet *peng*, he will be able to control you.

In explaining these concepts to my students, I like to use the construction metaphor of pouring concrete into forms. My frame is the form built to receive concrete—my opponent's energy. As my form receives it, the energy sinks to the bottom, stabilizing my form as it sets. To carry the analogy further, as the concrete sets, it expands evenly in all directions with unstoppable strength. This is the discharge phase of the cycle.

Using the *peng* structure and feeling to neutralize is fundamentally using the *yin* half of the vertical circle of the "threading the nine pearls" exercise. From the point of contact, usually the wrist or lower arms, you neutralize the energy by taking it down, joint by joint, through the elbows and shoulders, down the spine, and down the legs through hips, knees and ankles into the feet and the ground.

A frame is a posture with tension, and a posture is a frame without tension.

Pile Stance Wooden Man Exercise

Master Cai emphasized that the main thing in push-hands, whether fixed pattern or free style, is to be in control of your own centerline. "Because only if you control your own centerline, can you control your opponent's centerline." By control he means "keeping the three points aligned on a straight line." To review briefly, the three points are (1) the *baihui* on top of the head (2) the *huiyin* or perineum between anus and genitals and (3) any point between points no.2 and no.4 on the midline of the channel between the feet(*Fig 7.2*) .

To align these properly (1) the head must be held straight and the chin tucked; (2) the pelvis must be tucked under and upward and the abdomen pulled in so the

You only need to think about your *mingmen* and expand it to inflate your *peng* and even out your opponent's throughout your body.

Fig. 7.2 Three points on a straight line in archer step

lower back and *mingmen* (gate of life) is full and expanded; (3) the distribution of the weight on the feet should be **even**, whether in parallel or archer step. This does not mean that the weight distribution has to be **equal** (50-50) between the two feet, but simply that whatever weight there is on a foot must be distributed evenly as regards to inside and outside, as well as front (balls) and rear (heels) of the foot.

Master Cai's method of systematic push-hand training starts with the wooden man exercises in the pile stance. Having the feet parallel, as in the *wuji* standing position, makes the esential link between the *wuji* meditation and its application in the double exercises clear and direct. One person (A) holds the small *peng* posture with one forearm on top of the other, while the other person (B) holds the push posture and then puts his hands on A's arm.*(Fig. 7.3*Fig. 7.5 Changing hands 2Fig. 7.4 Changing hands 1)

B begins to push on A, exerting a slow and increasing pressure. Without collapsing his arms or otherwise changing form or moving, A receives B's strength and takes it down into his feet, turning his posture into a frame by becoming more *yang*, or substantial by precisely matching the strength of the energy received.

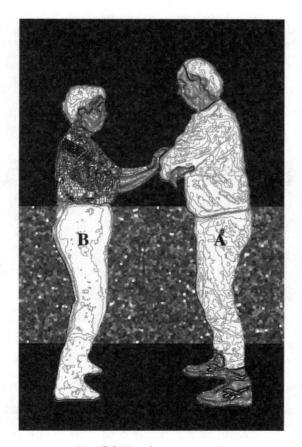

Master Cai's method of systematic push-hand training starts with the wooden man exercises in the pile stance. This makes the esential link between the *wuji* meditation and its application in the double exercises clear and direct.

Fig. 7.3 Wooden man exerise

It is important to remember that this is a cooperative training effort, not a competition. B gives A only as much strength as A is able to work with comfortably without collapsing or moving the centerline to the heels or leaning forward in compensation. Neither party should have any external movement of the arms or centerline. Use of the metaphor of concrete being poured into its form may be helpful here. Think of B's energy as the concrete being poured into the form which is A. The concrete flows from top to bottom ands sets up within the form an immovable and secure structure.

The length of the push is variable. In the beginning, it is better to have it longer and steadier, making it easier for the receiver to work with. I find it easy to coordinate the breath, so that a push lasts the length of an exhale. Later, after some skill has been acquired, the push can be quicker more abrupt and thus, more challenging.

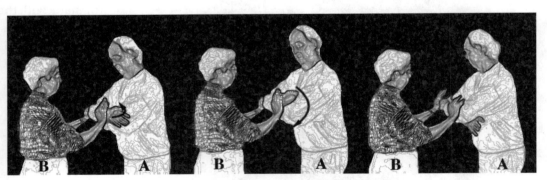

Fig. 7.4 Changing hands 1

After each push (breath), B lets up on the pressure on A, so that A can change arms. A changes arms in the following way. If the left hand is on top of the right one, curl the left hand toward the centerline. This allows the right forearm to circle to the outside and forward to be placed on top of the left forearm. *(Fig. 7.4)* Straighten out the left hand underneath the right elbow and, for structural integrity be sure that it is the *laogong* point of the right palm, and not just the fingers, which rests on the upper left arm just above the elbow . After the next push (breath),

Fig. 7.5 Changing hands 2

change back the other way. You now have a cycle going.

Now practice changing arms by circling them the opposite way to the inside. Again place the left forearm on top of the right one. Now curl or hook the right hand toward the centerline. This allows you to circle the right forearm inside towards the body and place it on top of the left one to receive the next push. *(Fig. 7.5)*

We systematically elaborate on this basic "wooden man" exercise, making it more complex in form while continuing to practice the same simple (though not easy) essence. Begin with A, the receiver, alternately extending the arms with each push. A's part in this is exactly like the solo exercise discussed in Chapter 5. From the small *peng* posture with left arm on top of the right one, A extends his

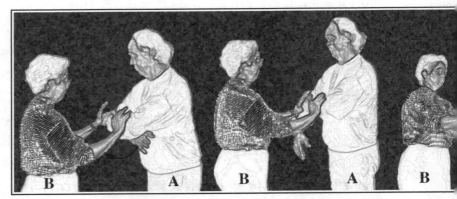

Fig. 7.6   Wooden man with folding-extending

right arm underneath the left arm of B as B pushes. When B lets up on the push, A , bending at the right elbow, puts the right hand on the left forearm, curls the left hand towards the centerline, circles the left forearm underneath the right and extends the left forearm underneath the right arm of B . Continue the cycle for a while and then trade positions.*(FIg. 7.6)*

Next, trade parts with every push, as follows.*(Fig. 7.7)* Beginning position: B pushes on A, who has his right arm extended underneath B's left arm . Then B folds from his push posture into small *peng* with his left forearm on top of the right. A unfolds from his single arm extended *peng* into push posture on B, putting his right hand on B's left wrist and his left hand on B's forearm just below the elbow. As A is doing this, B extends his right arm underneath A's left.

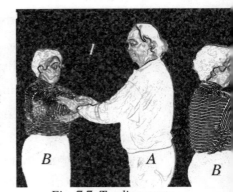

Fig. 7.7 Trading parts

After A has pushed once on

B, reverse the process. A folds from his push posture into small *peng* with his left forearm on top of the right. B unfolds from his single arm extended *peng* into push posture on A, putting his right hand on A's left wrist and his left hand on A's forearm just below the elbow. As B is doing this, A extends his right arm underneath B's left. Repeat cyclically for a while, and then reverse the hands, with both A and B folding the left forearm underneath the right in small *peng* and extending it underneath the other's right arm.

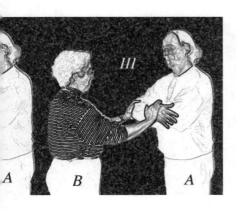

Next add the challenge of moving the feet with each push. Back up and start again with the simplest upper structure and gradually build up the complexity of the pattern. B pushes on A's small *peng,* except now both have their left foot in front of the right in a very small archer step . As B lets up on his push, both change feet, so that the right foot will be in front for the next push. In this exercise, the feet change, but the centerlines do not move; they stay in place. This means that the left foot takes a half-step back while the right foot advances a half-step. After the next push, the right foot takes a half step back while the left foot advances a half step. Both are actually walking in place.

Add all the elaborations of the arm movements described above one by one while continuing to move the feet. Each player alternately extends left and right forearms in turn while the other is pushing on him . Then the players alternate pushing and receiving.

> In fact, Master Cai likens the wooden man exercise to pile driving; just like a pile that is being driven in the ground, you take the energy that is exerted on you down the centerline into the ground to stabilize and sink your own structure.

It is no accident that the basic Wooden Man exercise is done in the pile stance, as the *wuji* stance is also sometimes called. In fact, Master Cai likens the wooden man exercise to pile driving; just like a pile that is being driven in the ground, you take the energy that is exerted on you down the centerline into the ground to stabilize and sink your own structure.

Iniitally, the pusher should not exert too much strength, but slowly increase it so that the receiver can practice being even and detecting unevenness in his opponent as well as himself. Both pusher and receiver should pay strict attention to prevent leaning forward with the centerline.

You can actually make a game out of this. If the receiver feels the pusher leaning in his push, he can withdraw his frame to cause him to lose his balance. Likewise , if the pusher senses the receiver leaning forward and bracing himself in anticipation, the pusher does not push causing the receiver to lose his balance.

In the intermediate level of practice, the pusher can push more abruptly and with greater strength. However, the ultimate direction of the exercise is to make it softer as the perception becomes keener. This way the following becomes ever smoother until finally it will be an exercise of pure yi (awareness/intention) and not *li* and *qi*. (strength).

One student asked Master Cai the pertinent question: wasn't the "wooden man exercise" practicing resistance in opposition to the often stated *taiji* principle in the classics to "never resist" and "always yield." Master Cai replied that what the classics mean by resistance is the unconscious use of strength, whereas what is learned in the "wooden man" exercise is the conscious use of substantiality, fullness or integration, as opposed to the insubstantiality and emptiness of relaxation or *song (sung)*. True *taiji*, he stressed, is the proper balance between empty and full, *yin* and *yang*, and knowing when and how to use each.

What is learned in the "wooden man" exercise is the conscious use of substantiality, fullness or integration, as opposed to the insubstantiality and emptiness of relaxation or *song (sung)*

In this connection, as we will see, the frame has both defensive and offensive uses. Defensively it is used as a last resort. When all possibilities of neutralizing have been exhausted, you protect your body and centerline by giving the opponent your frame and allowing him to discharge on it, causing you to jump or hop backwards while maintaining the centerline. Offensively, the "wooden man" frame is the basis for the ability to *fajin (fa chin)* or discharge energy.

Two-Person Vertical Circle Exercise

In the following double exercises, we use the "wooden man" principles to illustrate Master Cai's fundamental techniques of neutralizing and discharging using the vertical circle. In *Fig. 7.8* A and B face each other in the archer stance, with either the left or right foot forward. A assumes the "ward-off" and "press" posture while B assumes the double push posture on A's forward arm.

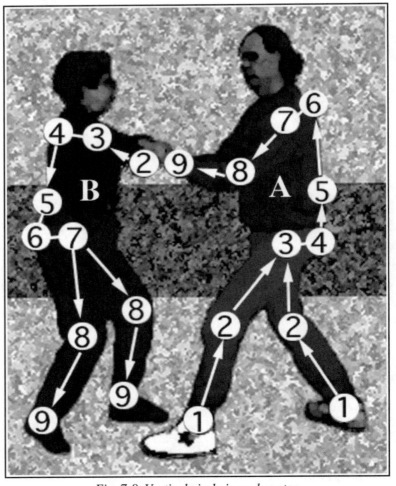

Fig. 7-8 Vertical circle in archer step

Chapter 7 Using Energy and Strength in Partnered Practices

Using the nine pearls technique of enumerating the joints as the energy moves through them, B starts by pushing from the rear foot, feeling the energy move up the leg through the ankle, knee and hips, up the spine from the lower, middle and upper spines and down the arms through to shoulders, elbows and wrist, and winds up by exerting a slow, steady and light force on A's arm. Again, it cannot be overemphasized that in the beginning, sudden and great forces are counterproductive and destroy the value of the exercise. A, responding to B's push, holds the frame of his *peng* steady, matching precisely the strength of B's push. A neither uses excess nor insufficient force, maintaining a minimum distance of a spread-out hand between palm and chest.

A absorbs, or neutralizes, B's force by relaxing (sinking) internally and "opening" the right side of the body, turning out the right knee, hip and shoulder slightly, as in the solo exercises in chapter 4. It is as if the body is a hinge, with the centerline the pin. The left side of the body is stable like the half of the hinge screwed into the doorframe. The right side of the hinge is moveable, and like the door, opens upon being pushed. In fact, by this sinking and opening, A neutralizes B's force and takes it down into the rear leg and foot. In this neutralizing half of the vertical circle, A again enumerates the "nine pearls" of the joints as the energy moves through the wrists, elbows, shoulders, upper back, middle back, lower back, hips, knees, ankles into the ground.

After neutralizing B's force by "opening", A returns it and discharges his own *jin*, or integral force, by "closing"; the right side of the body turns back to its original position.

> It cannot be overemphasized that in the beginning, sudden and great forces are counterproductive and destroy the value of the exercise.

The right knee, hip and shoulder square again with the front foot. Pushing from the sole of the right foot and straightening the rear leg, A feels the energy coming up his leg, moves it up the spine by expanding the *mingmen*, and by expanding the upper back beween the shoulders propels it down the right arm and out the right palm pressing the left wrist towards B. In this discharging half of the vertical circle, A again enumerates the nine pearls of the joints as the energy moves through them, this time in the opposite direction, from foot to hand. As B receives A's energy, it is B's turn to neutralize by sinking internally and opening, taking A's energy down the nine pearls into the foot, and then discharging by sending the energy back up again.

We have here a highly internalized exercise of continuous energy cycling between two people. To really experience it properly, it is important not to have any external movement of the frame (including the hands and arms), nor any forward and backward movement of the centerline. The only movement permitted is the very slight rotational movement of the centerline and knees in opening and closing.

To reiterate, in the beginning, work with very small energies. Even so, when done properly, you will be surprised at how exhausting this work is. In the intermediate stage, when enough feeling and strength have been developed to maintain the frame, you can gradually increase the amount of force exerted, developing it into an intensely isometric partnered exercise. In the advanced stage of practice, go back to practicing again very lightly, practicing the feeling and awareness, instead of the strength.

> We have here a highly internalized exercise of continuous energy cycling between two people. To really experience it properly, it is important not to have any external movement of the frame nor any forward and backward movement of the centerline.

158

Two-Person Horizontal Circle Exercise

Fig. 7.9 ilustrates a simple partnered or double exercise Master Cai taught us to develop awareness of the flow of energy through the horizontal circle. A assumes the basic *peng* posture of holding the sphere. B assumes the push posture and puts one hand on A's wrist and the other just below the elbow. Or, if A's hands are separated, B puts one hand on each of A's wrists. B starts the cycle by putting a small intention of pushing energy in one of his palms, say the left, which is pushing on the right wrist of A. It must be emphasized here that there should be no physical movement, only intention and energy.

First A fills, or makes substantial, his *peng* only in enough to match B's energy and absorb it into his frame. Then A neutralizes B's energy by taking it around in a horizontal circle and returns it to B's right palm. To train awareness of this process, A, at first aloud and then to himself, enumerates the seven joints of wrist, elbow, shoulder, spine, shoulder, elbow, wrist as he feels the energy passing through them. When the energy reaches A's left wrist, it is B's turn to receive and cycle the energy in a horizontal circle and enumerate his joints as the energy passes through them: (right) wrist, elbow, shoulder, spine, shoulder, elbow, (left) wrist. Then it is A's turn again.

After getting the hang of it doing it one way, introduce all the possible variations. First, reverse the direction of the energy flow in a continuous circle going the other way. Then, reverse directions at random by sending the

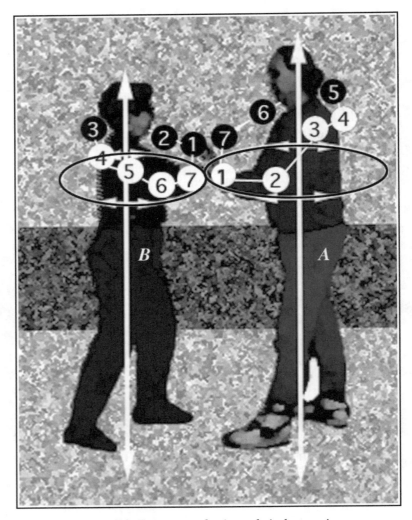

Fig. 7.9 Two-person horizontal circle exercise

Practice the basic centerline movements and their combinations while at the same time increasing the level of *qi* energy until it becomes concentrated as *li* or purely physical strength.

energy back immediately by the recieving hand rather than cycling it through the horizontal circle to the other hand. Of course, first start out with the feet in parallel stance. Later do the exercise with feet in archer step with weight 50-50, varying it with more weight on the rear and then more on the front.

Working with Strength

In the following exercises the polarity of stillness and movement interacts with the energy-strength continuum of *qi* and *li*. We practice the basic centerline movements and their combinations while at the same time increasing the level of *qi* energy until it becomes concentrated as *li* or purely physical strength. The purpose of this is to increase the integrity of our sphere and its integration with the centerline and foundation. That is to say, increase the substance of our *peng*.

Working with internal or isometric strength, both in solo and partnered work, is indispensable for the realization of *jin*, or explosive force. It must be approached with both intelligence and diligence, lest development becomes stuck, unable to transcend *li*, the level of pure strength, to the level of *jin* or explosive force, then to the level of *yi* , the level of intention, and finally to the level of *shen* , the level of the spirit.

The centerline, strictly speaking, can move only in three ways, as determined by the polarities of our body in space and gravity. It can be moved up or down; it can be shifted back and forth from foot to foot; and it can be rotated clockwise or counterclockwise. From these three primal polarites, an infinite number of permutations and combinations allow for an unlimited number of movements. But whatever the movement, the intent or purpose is always and only to neutralize your opponent's attacking energy.

The centerline, strictly speaking, can move only in three ways, as determined by the polarities of our body in space and gravity. It can be moved up or down; it can be shifted back and forth from foot to foot; and it can be rotated clockwise or counterclockwise.

Remember when you are working in these partnered exercises to keep your movements to an absolute minimum and internalized as much as possible.

Neutralizing by Shifting

Assume *peng* posture in archer step while your partner assumes the push posture on your ward-off . Be still and neutralize his force down into your root while he slowly increases the strength of his push. When you get to the point where, in the stillness of stationary *peng*, you cannot neutralize your opponent's force anymore by taking his energy down into your root, then you must not yield to the temptation to use strength and resist him. Instead, you must yield to his force and neutralize it by allowing yourself to be pushed back. In this shifting back of the centerline it is important to maintain the body as an integrated unit, that is, you must not allow the integrity of the sphere to break or collapse. *(fig.7.10)*

At first, as you are being pushed back and the weight is shifted onto the rear leg, feel your opponent's pressure carried through the body down to the knee. You neutralize by physically bending and opening the rear knee. The saying is that "bending the knee carries the hip," meaning that bending the knee allows the hip to relax which enables you to take your opponent's *qi* into your feet.

As you get more advanced in the art of neutralizing, you will no longer need to bend and open the knee physically. You can keep it physically straight and only relax it internally with the mind (awareness) to take your opponent's energy down into your feet.

Fig. 7.10 Neutralizing by shifting

Don't allow yourself to be shifted back further than the fourth point, unless your opponent's force is so great that it becomes necessary. Your structure will become unstable and you will then need to take a step to reestablish it.

Neutralizing by Rotation

If your opponent's force is greater than can be neutralized by mere shifting and opening the knee, then you add the actions of sinking and rotating your centerline. In the beginning, when pushed back to the fourth point, you first sink a little to stabilize yourself, and then, as a seperate action, you open the knee and rotate the centerline to neutralize. As you get more advanced, the sinking and centerline rotation become one simultaneous movement.

There is a right way and a wrong way of using the shifting and opening technique of neutralizing. Most people do it the wrong way; that is, they first turn out the knee to open and then they shift the centerline back. The correct way is to first shift back and take the opponent's

Fig. 7.11 Neutralizing by rotation

energy into your center, and then open to neutralize by turning out the knee. This way provides a continous circle for neutralizing and discharging, while the wrong way breaks it up into two discontinuous and opposing semi-circles.

After mastering the technique of "opening" by turning half the body, the next higher level of training involves "opening" by turning the entire body as an integrated unit. *(Fig. 7.11)* This allows the neutralization of yet even greater forces. Thus when B pushes on A, A turns the entire body, including the left (front) hip, shoulder and arm. The important thing here is that the left shoulder and arm stay in the same position relative to the body; it is the torso that moves them; they do not move independently. Thus, the essential structure is maintained. Great forces can easily be neutralized and returned as discharge because only a slight turning of the body cylinder can effectively deflect a large force aimed at it.

As proficiency in this double exercise improves, the amount of force exerted by B's push can gradually be increased. This will allow A to add the other elements of neutralization and discharge to his response, namely the sinking, raising, and shifting back and forth movements of his centerline.

A's response should always be exactly proportional to B's force. As B increases the strength of his push, A will respond and neutralize by opening further (although never exceeding the 45 degree limit), sinking and shifting back. As a consequence B will always be thrown back by the exact amount of force he exerted.

If the force of B's push exceeds A's capacity to neutralize it by merely "opening," A will employ either or both by sinking and shifting back to accommodate it and increase his capacity for neutralization. First, practice sinking the centerline in response to increased force, then practice shifting back.

Again notice that while the front knee is allowed to go backward and forward in shifting, it is not allowed to collapse inward because it would destroy the integrity of the structure and result in a loss of centerline and balance.

Chapter 8

Using Movement & Stillness To Neutralize

The Uses of Stillness and Movement

In the meditative martial arts, the uses of movement are limited and subject to strict restrictions. First, movement is limited to defense or neutralization, and complete stillness is required for offense, or the discharge of energy.

Used defensively, movement is also subject to the following restrictions: (1) You move only as much as you need to, in accordance with the old saying that "small movement is better than big movement, and no movement is better than small movement." (2) You never initiate any movement. Strictly speaking do not move yourself, but allow yourself to be moved by your opponent into an advantageous position.

In Master Cai's system, stillness, as opposed to movement, predominates. Stillness allows better cultivation of both stability and awareness. For awareness and stability, the best practice is standing still.

Movement is practiced basically for the opening of the joints and stretching of the muscles and ligaments. In actual use, however, no movement is used in discharging energy and movement is used only for neutralizing, and even then it is minimized.

> **Movement is limited to defense or neutralization; offense, or the discharge of energy, requires complete stillness.**

Nine Pearls Double Exercise

1. In *Fig. 8.1* A and B both assume archer stance with the left foot forward and the weight 50-50. A expands, pushes forward with *ji* energy on B's *peng* posture (single or double ward-off).

Fig. 8.1 Four energies double exercise

2. B shifts his centerline back to the fourth point, sinks and opens to neutralize with *lu* energy, dropping his hands in a semicircle, and taking A's energy down into his rear, right foot.

3. B simultaneously begins to square and close the hips and shift the centerline forward to the no. 2 point while circling his arms and hands up to take his opponent A up with *peng* energy. While taking A up, B's middle finger points upward to direct the intention and energy.

4. Once forward and up, B takes A down to mid-torso level with *an* energy. Executing this manuever, B must be careful to keep his centerline on the no. 2 point above the front foot and not shift it back to the rear foot. Note that B's rear leg bends a little to provide spring.

5. Lastly, B pushes A forward by expanding with *ji* energy by means of straightening the rear leg and filling his *mingmen*.

6. Now it is A's turn to do a cycle of *peng, an, lu,* and *ji*. Absorbing B's forward expansion *(ji)* with *lu* energy, A

170

shifts his centerline back to the fourth point, sinks and opens to neutralize with *lu* energy, dropping his hands in a semicircle, and taking B's energy down into his rear, right foot.

7. A simultaneously begins to square and close the hips and shift the centerline forward to no. 2 point while circling his arms and hands up to take his opponent B up with *peng* energy. While taking B up, A's middle finger points upward to direct the intention and energy.

8. Once forward and up, A takes B down to mid-torso level with *an* energy. Executing this manuever, A must be careful to keep his centerline on the no. 2 point above the front foot and not shift it back to the rear foot. Note that A's rear leg bends a little to provide spring.

9. Lastly, A pushes B forward, expanding with *ji* energy by straightening the rear leg and filling his *mingmen.* Now the cycle starts all over again with another turn for B.

Description of Circle Pushing

In the "nine pearls" double exercise the partners take turns doing the entire vertical circle of *peng, an, lu,* and *ji* sequentially. In the traditional *taiji* push-hands cycle demonstrated in *(Fig. 8.2)*, each energy is neutralized by the opponent's use of another energy in the following manner.

1. Shifting forward, A throws a left punch to B, or attempts to push him. B raises his right arm in ward-off while shifting back to neutralize.

2-3. By grabbing A's left wrist with his left hand and controlling A's left elbow with his right arm, B rotates left and closes to execute *lu* (roll-back) in counterattack.

4. A neutralizes B's roll-back by *ji* (pressing) his right hand on his own left arm and closes by rotating left to counter B's intent.

5. As he does so, A pulls back his right forearm, folding it underneath his left forearm in small *peng* .

6. B then responds and neutralizes A's *ji* (press) by *an,* pushing down with both hands on A's left arms and pushing him back.

7-9. Then the cycle repeats: A neutralizes B's push by shifting back with his *peng* and while doing so, grabs B's elbow with his left hand and B's right wrist with his right hand, ready to rotate and execute roll-back. B neutralizes A's rollback by pressing; A neutralizes B's press by pushing ; B neutralizes A's push by roll-back, etc....

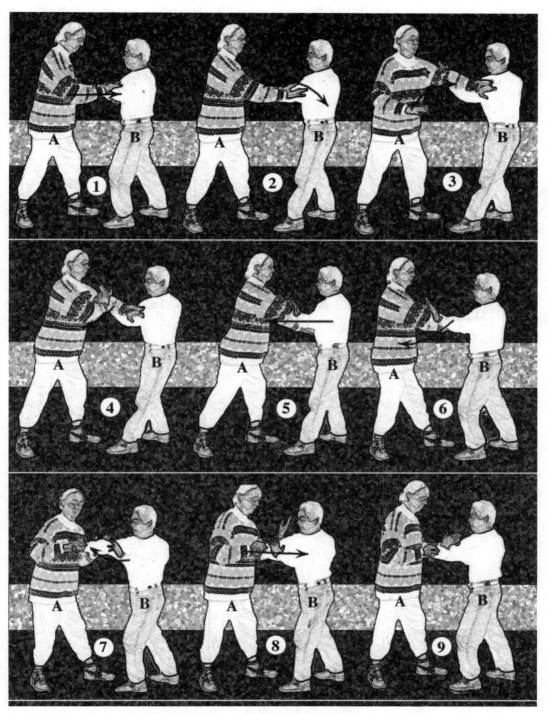

Fig. 8. 2 Four energies push-hands pattern

As described here, the cycle moves in a clockwise direction from the point of view of A and counterclockwise direction from the point of view of B. The direction of movement can, however, be reversed at anytime by either party, regardless of which foot is forward. In *(Fig. 8.3)*

Your *peng* (frame) is filled with feeling, with awareness.

1-2. B is executing *lu* or rollback on A's right arm.

3-4. A responds by applying *ji* or pressing energy of left palm on the inside of the right elbow and folding his right arm to present B with a small peng, or closed frame.

5-6. B neutralizes A's *ji* or pressing energy by applying *an* or push energy.

7-9. A neutralizes B's push by executing *lu* or rollback by circling his right arm underneath to control B's left arm, and rotating open.

Here is a good technique for reversing the direction of circling. When you are in the small *peng* position with one forearm folded underneath the other. Say the right arm is underneath. To continue the circle in the same direction, you extend the underneath right arm to control the left elbow of your opponent and shift back to execute rollback on the left side . To reverse the direction of the circle, you grab the right wrist of your opponent from underneath, and then shift back to execute rollback on the right side.

In *Fig. 8.4 ,1-3* demonstrates Master Cai's push-hand technique of first turning the palm inward towards the chest before extending the arm. This is really a palm change Master Cai took from *baguachang* which he

Fig. 8.3 Changing Direction of circling in pushhands

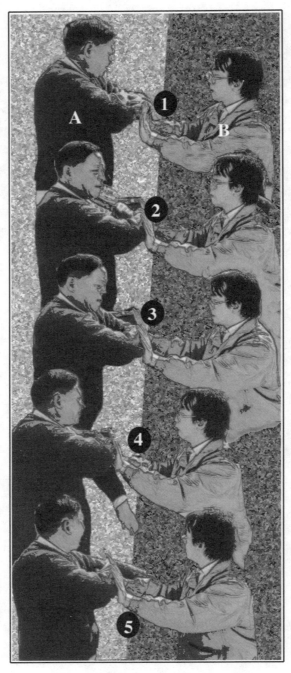

Fig. 8.4 Turning the palm inward

considers superior to *taijiquan* in *yin-yang* changes. *Baquachang* allows the centerline to turn much more internally, around a much tighter axis, than *taiji* because turning the palm in makes the turning radius of the centerline is shorter than is standard in the *taiji* method where you just extend the arm.

When working by yourself, always use this method for practice. In actual push-hands, this technique is used when you have been maneuvered into a position where your sphere is so small that it needs to be strengthened to prevent its collapse and you cannot circle the outside way.

Fig. 8.4 , 4-5. After circling the palm, the forearm extends. As it extends, follow the path of the energy with your awareness. First the forearm makes contact with your opponent's wrist and then that point of contact moves up your opponent's arm and down your own arm as your arm extends and points towards him.

When you extend the hand and forearm in continuous push-hands circling, your palm will be facing down and aimed at the side of your opponents body. But, when you intend to discharge, the palm will turn sideways and the energy will be aimed directly at your opponent's centerline.

Of course, these are not the only options for using the extended arm. As your arm extends underneath his arm, you can put intention forward into your opponent's armpit to uproot him.

Evenness in your *peng* will give you the readiness to discharge instantaneously. Any uneven distribution of tension in the frame will lead to double weightedness and loss of centerline control.

You can put your hand on your opponent's upper arm and move him sideways with the rotation of your centerline and frame. If he responds to this by resisting, then execute *lu* (rollback) on him by rotating hand and forearm while rotating your centerline and sphere, thus drawing him into yourself, and then apply *ji* (press) with the other hand on palm to discharge him and throw him away.

Neutralizing in Free Play

In push-hands, whether fixed pattern or freestyle, always strive to maintain the integrity of your own structure. Do not get fixated on trying to push your opponent. It is of secondary importance. Only when you are comfortable within your own frame and can keep your centerline will you be able to have true control of the situation.

The principle of relative motion refers to the fact that even if you need to move, you never move more than one part of your body at the same time.

While this is simple, it isn't easy. In the heat of an exchange, it's all too easy to forget the centerline and forget to keep the frame. And while moving, it's imperative to keep the frame filled, because if you collapse, you will lose your integration. As the saying goes, "if you lose it, you can't use it."

And although your *peng* (frame) is filled, it isn't heavy because it is filled only with awareness. In push-hands, you practice staying light and even in your contact. The lighter the touch you can maintain, the better your martial art will be. The heavier you are, the more your opponent will be able to take advantage of and control you. Only with a lightness of touch can there be listening sensitivity and following ability. Besides lightness, the other quality your frame must have is evenness. Evenness in your *peng* will give you the readiness to discharge instantaneously. Any uneven distribution of tension in the frame leads to being heavy (double weighted) and losing centerline control. Thus when you are even and you detect an uneven place in your opponent, you can enter the hole and discharge. Conversely, if you push him in an uneven fashion, and he does not even out your push, he cannot push you. But if he makes it even, then he can discharge on you.

Either you keep your centerline steady and move the points of contact or you keep the points of contact steady and move your centerlineline.

In neutralizing, Master Cai employs a variety of techniques which are organized in a loose hierarchy of usage, depending on the skill of the opponent and the strength of the force to be neutralized. Generally speaking, he will first neutralize by moving the sphere independently from the centerline which remains still. If that is insufficient, he will neutralize by connecting the sphere to the centerline and then rotating them together as a unit. If that is insufficient, he will add shifting the centerline back before rotating. Then, if necessary, he will add stepping. Finally, as a last resort, he will use hopping. We will consider each in turn.

Neutralizing in free play, your sphere changes shape as you follow the direction of the movement of your opponent, going up or down when he goes up or down, forward and backward as he comes in or withdraws. The better your *gong fu* skill, the more adjustments you make

In neutralizing you should move as little as possible. How much you move should be a function of (1) your skill and (2) the amount of force exerted on you by the opponent.

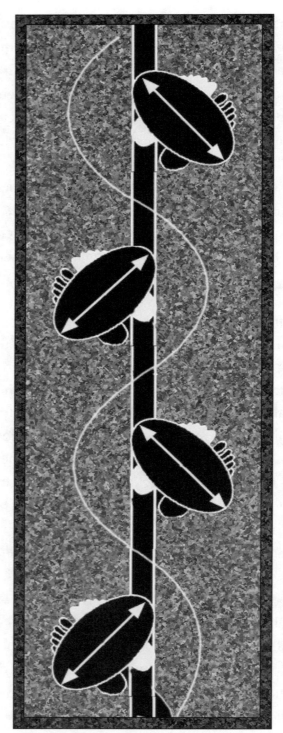

Fig. 8.5 Walking backward in neutralizing

Chapter 8 Using Movement and Stillness in Neutralization

in your basic *peng* or ball(oon) structure to absorb/ neutralize your opponent's energies.

While there are no rules for freestyle pushing, you should strive, in the beginning, to keep the arms connected, forming an integrated circle which, in neutralizing, rotates around the centerline in a hulahoop fashion, horizontally or diagonally, as explained in Chapter 5, when we discussed the structure of the sphere. Later, when you acquire more skill in controlling your centerline, keeping it steady and still, you can disengage and separate the arms and move them separately to neutralize and control your opponent,as in executing roll-back.

Any tension is a loss of awareness; any gain in awareness is an increase in relaxation.

In neutralizing with the rotation of the connected sphere, must keep the shoulders and hips aligned while the centerline turns. The spine does not twist; the rotation is done solely with the waist. Of course, when you're using centerline rotation, you can also employ the diagonal circle of alternating elbows to augment the neutralization. In that case, as you rotate and relax the *kua (k'ua)*, or hip to neutralize, let the corresponding elbow dip down to help neutralize. In Master Cai's words, "let the hip lead the elbow".

If your opponent is aggresively advancing while pushing on you, you may need to neutralize and control him while walking backwards. You do this by walking backward in an "s" or figure eight type pattern.*(Flig 8.5)* First take him to one side by stepping and rotating the centerline, then with the next step, go to the other side and rotate the centerline the other way, changing hands as needed.

The Principle of Relative Motion

Even when movement is used, as in neutralizing, stillness still governs it under the category of "relative motion". The principle of relative motion refers to the fact that even if you need to move, you never move more than one part of your body at the same time. Keep the rest of the body as stable and still as you can. Then your movement will be as efficient as possible. The reason is obvious: All joints connect two bones. If you want to move with maximum stability and effciency, keep one bone stable, so the other can move.

The *taiji* attitude is to be negative in a positive way, whereas external systems are positive in a negative way.

For example, in the foundation. If you want to move the part of the body above the knees as an integrated unit, then you must keep the knees and what is below them fixed to provide a stable point of reference for the movement. If you allow the knees and legs below them to move, your movement will lack integration, stability and awareness because the conscious mind is still limited and cannot really keep track of more than one simple movement at a time. As Master Cai summed it up, "In order to have relative motion, you must fix one point; if you want to move the knee, fix the ankle; if you want to move the hip, fix the knee; if you want to turn the waist (centerline), fix the hips; if you want to move the hand, fix the elbow; if you want to move the elbow; fix the shoulder." In this way, stillness is integrated within movement.

One very important example of the principle of relative motion is the relationship between the center and the periphery of our human sphere or cylinder. Again, in Master Cai's words, "If you want to move the outside or periphery, you must fix the center. Or, vice versa, if you want to move the center or the inside, you must stabilize and fix the outside periphery."

Applying this to push-hands or fighting practice, you can use the principle of relative motion to change the relationship between your centerline and your opponent's in one of two ways. Either you keep your centerline steady and move the points of contact around, as in circling with the sphere and arms. Or you can keep the points of contact steady and move your centerline, either through external repositioning, stepping or walking but preferably through subtle internal adjustments of shifting and rotation.

Neutralizing is *yin* and involves the practice of "opening", sinking and shifting backwards of the centerline. These can only be mastered to the extent that we develop *song* or relaxation with awareness.

The importance of being still and remaining integrated while moving is most important. Movement without integration results in diminishing stability and awareness because our conscious mind can't really keep track simultaneously of all the components that constitute complex movement.

In neutralizing you should move as little as possible. How much you move should be a function of (1) your skill and (2) the amount of force exerted on you by the opponent. Any excessive movement on your part can be used by your opponent against you. What is most desirable in neutralizing is maintaining external stillness in your posture and your centerline while internally shifting, sinking and rotating your centerline very subtly to change the direction of the attacking force. That's how you change to your advantage the relationship of your own centerline to your opponent's centerline .

To sum up: following the classics, Master Cai's push-hands is based on the *yin-yang* principle. Neutralizing is *yin* and involves the practice of "opening", sinking and shifting backwards of the centerline. These can only be mastered to the extent that we develop *song* or relaxation with awareness. Both of these are cultivated interdependently. We can increase our awareness only through learning *song* (relaxation), and we can learn to relax only by growing in awareness. Any tension is a loss of awareness; any gain in awareness is an increase in relaxation.

Master Cai never tires of reiterating and exhorting us to minimize our obsession with discharging our energy and in our practice emphasize our ability to listen to and follow our opponents. As our awareness and ability to neutralize grows, the ability to discharge correctly will automatically result.

When your opponent moves, touches and fills you, immediately neutralize and probe for his center with your *yi* or awareness in order to detect vacancies or points of blocked *qi*.

Advanced Methods of Neutralization

After you have thoroughly programmed your body to neutralize with half the vertical circle of threading the nine pearls, you can practice the more advanced method of neutralzing by splitting your opponents energy in your center. In this method, when you are attacked, again do not resist, but instead of taking your opponent's energy into your root, take it into your center and then split his energy. You simultaneously sink half of it down into your

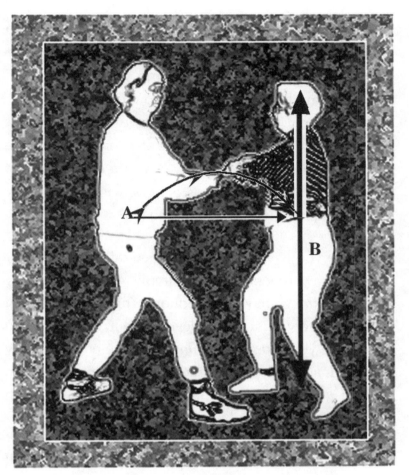

..."borrowing energy" is a very high stage of development where you can neutralize your opponent's *jin* (explosive energy) solely with your awaress.

Fig. 8.6 Neutralizing by splitting the opponent's energy

root to neutralize him, and raise half of it up your own centerline in order to take his force up and uproot him. *(Fig. 8.6)*

Master Cai said there are two ways of neutralizing. The first is to use your own *qi* (energy) to neutralize. The second and superior method is to absorb your opponent's energy, borrow it and return it to him (with interest, if so desired)."Absorption is the highest stage of neutralization", Master Cai said. It is used when there is no time for either rotating or shifting. This method is predicated on the fact that every point on the body, every cell, can be *yin* or *yang*, and can neutralize or discharge. When every cell of the body simultaneously absorbs your opponent's force, a great econmy is achieved, because the energy no longer has to follow any of the complicated pathways of the body. Because the whole body is aware of the point of contact, the neutralization is achieved instantaneously and simultaneously throughout the body.

Even before making physical contact, be sure your eyes and your *yi* (awareness) control your opponent's centerline before they move.

Once you have received and neutralized his energy with your awareness, then you simply redirect his energy back to him with your intention. This is "borrowing energy", a very high stage of development, where you can neutralize your opponent's *jin* (explosive energy) solely with your awaress, and redirect it back to him solely with your *yi* (intention). He literally throws himself away with his own energy, like a ball bouncing off a wall..

This means that in *taiji* your body must be *yin* at all times, that is to say, ready to receive your opponent's energy as opposed to other systems which are *yang*, always putting out their own energy. The *taiji* attitude is to be negative in a positive way, whereas external systems are positive in a negative way.

Strategies in Pushhands

When you play push-hands with people from different schools, you should first ascertain, before you decide to

discharge on them, whether or not they have developed
a frame and do hopping practice. If they don't, you should
only neutralize but not discharge on them, for they could
be hurt. But you won't necessarely be rewarded for this
kindness. Many times, these people will go away with the
wrong impression, thinking you are unable to discharge
and spread stories accordingly. This is particularly evident
in so-called "noodle style" push-hands practitioners who,
weaving, bending and twisting any which way, neutralize
without principle, meaning they never keep the centerline.

Do not attack your opponent's weakness locally, for then you will lose your own centerline. Instead, follow and enter globally.

The main objective of this "noodle style" of push-
hands seems to be to hang on to the piece of real estate
their feet are occupying, violating all postural consider-
ations and in the process, disintegrating their centerline
from the foundation. In Master Cai's words "It is no use.
They may be difficult to move, but they are easy to hurt.
Therefore, do not discharge on them."

When you play with noodle style practitioners, do not
play their game, play your own game. Too much following is no good. Master Cai advocates to "just probe and
move into their center with your intention and integration". As their form and *qi* collapses, your intention will
reach their center and you will create resistance. Then you
use intention to move them.

When you are playing with practitioners of other
martial systems, such as *yongchun (yung ch'un, wing
chun)*, you should always follow the advice of the *taiji*
Classics and wait for them to make the first move. Even
before making physical contact, however, you should be

sure your eyes and your *yi* (awareness) control their centerline before they move, and then, put your awareness (attention/intention) in your hand for *peng*.

When they move, touch and fill you, immediately neutralize and probe for their center with your *yi* or awareness in order to detect vacancies or points of blocked *qi*. In other words, try to induce resistance and frame. When you feel the resistance, then you know you can discharge, or better yet, you can use your *yi* to transform and use the resistance to let them throw themselves.

It is important, however, that if and when you detect a vacancy or broken *qi* point, to not attack it locally, for then you will lose your own centerline. Instead, follow and enter globally. Make centerline contact through the sphere and then discharging on his weakness through his center. This doesn't mean you can't enter a hole you find; it only means you must enter it with your centerline.

When you make contact with your opponent, try to do it in a way that is advantageous to you, so you won't have to shift the point of contact to get a better one. Remember that if he is skilled, your opponent will be able to follow and take advantage of any movement that you instigate. If you do need to change the point of contact, do so with the palm change, that is the rotation of the forearm while maintaining the integrity of your circle and sphere.

Chapter 9

Levels of Awareness and Development

Master Cai's Use Of Stillness

Just as the use of movement with relaxation and attention characterizes the art of neutralizing energy, it is the use of stillness with integration and intention that defines the art of discharging energy.

At the higher levels of physical interaction, Master Cai is completely still, having internalized all exterior movement. Neutralization and discharge of energy are accomplished by consciousness alone: awareness (attention) to neutralize, intention to discharge. The great advantage is obvious. The time period for physical response to be completed is eliminated. The response is instantaneous. At the very moment Master Cai is touched, he is capable of repelling his opponent with devastating force without moving himself. This is dramatically illustrated in the photographs in *(Figs 9.1 and 9.2)* where the opponent being repelled is a blur of motion, while Master Cai's image remains crisp and clear.

The use of stillness with integration and intention defines the art of discharging energy.

I'll testify from both personal experience and observation. Untold numbers of highly qualified representatives from all conceivable martial arts disciplines, internal and external, Chinese, Japanese, Korean and European, have tried to kick, punch, or shove him. Never did I see anyone of them come close to executing their intentions before being neutralized and thrown back. Master Cai's awareness is so great that while he always waits for his opponent to initiate the attack, his own response is completed before his opponent's action is completed. As he put it in his own words "you start first, but I arrive and finish first."

Fig. 9.1 Master Cai's use of stillness in discharging

The *wuji-taiji* way seeks to increase the body's spectrum of relaxation-tension by working to extend both extremes.

Cultivating *Jin*

A word must be said about the relationship of *qi*, *li* and *jin*. *Qi*, of course, refers to the life energy that animates us. The more *qi* we have, generally, the healthier and stronger we are, both physically and constitutionally. *Li* and *jin* are two terms denoting strength. Both *li* and *jin* are dependent on *qi*. The more *qi* we have, the more *li* and *jin* we will have. Nevertheless, *li* and *jin* represent two very different types of strength. *Li* is a broad spectrum bulldozing kind of strength, such as is used in pushing a car or refrigerator. *Jin* is a very fast and sharply focussed,

Chapter 9 Using Stillness and Integration to Discharge Energy

Jin **is a very fast and sharply focussed, explosive kind of strength, such as is found in the energy of a cracking whip.**

Fig. 9.2 Master Cai's use of stillness in discharging

explosive kind of strength, such as found in the energy of a cracking whip.

A discharge of *jin* involves going instantaneously from a state of total relaxation to a state of total tension. The *wuji-taiji* way seeks to increase the body's spectrum of relaxation-tension by working to extend both extremes. On the one hand, through the practice of *wujii* meditation we affect deepening relaxation while heightening awareness. Paradoxically, by developing deeper and deeper relaxation, we increase the explosive power of our *jin* discharge. On the other hand, working with *li* and isometric principles increases the strength of our muscles, tendons and bones. In this way we work at extending the relaxation-tension spectrum of our body's musculature.

In the progression of your practice, you will typically start practice slowly by yourself; then you will practice slowly with one or many partners. Then you practice fast discharge by yourself; and finally, you practice fast discharge with a partner (and then only if that partner has a frame and knows the hopping technique of neutralizing).

Neutralize by Hopping with the Frame

By keeping the centerline and discharging our energy into the ground in successive hops, we maintain our center and remain unhurt.

Even before being taught how to produce and use integral force, the student must learn how to receive it and not be damaged by it. In the following exercise you will learn and practice hopping as the technique for maintaining the centerline and integration while being pushed by an opponent.

In the archer step, as the energy is discharged by A into B's pushing frame, B does not neutralize by sinking and opening, but, by keeping his frame filled at the same low level, allows himself to be moved as a unit by hopping back a step.

However, in hopping, there is no stepping; the relationship between the feet remains the same. That is, if the left foot is the front foot before the hop, it remains the front foot after the hop; it does not step back to become the rear foot. In the hop, the front foot will touch down first and discharge most of the energy received into the ground,

194

then the rear foot will touch down and the archer step is reestablished with the frame intact.*(Figs 9.3)*

Once again, at first, practice with small push energies and small hops backwards. Gradually, the force of the discharge can be increased. Correspondingly, the number of hops and the distance hopped will increase to accommodate the increased force of the pushes.

Fig. 9.3 Neutralize by hopping with frame

Hopping with a frame is a very important skill to learn. It is the last line of defense. When we have exhausted all our techniques of neutralizing incoming forces and our opponent is about to control our centerline and penetrate into the body, we stiffen our body into a frame and allow him to discharge his energy into our frame. Although this will throw us back physically, it will allow us to keep our centerline and discharge his energy into the ground in successive hops. And we maintain our center and remain unhurt.

So don't be overly concerned with defending the little territory on which you're standing. If you do, you're asking to get hurt. It is far better to be thrown back in the correct posture , i.e. integrated and with control of the centerline, than to stand your ground with an incorrect posture, i.e. disintegrated with loss of control of the centerline. Giving up the territory by hopping is a small price to pay for maintaining control over our centerline, and denying our opponent our body as a target for his discharge.

In the first stage, we learn to cultivate awareness of the internal structure of the human sphere as it functions in neutralizing and discharging physical energy.

First Level: Integration & Cylindricality

As in neutralization, Master Cai defines four levels of accomplishment in the art of discharging. These successive stages are characterized by decreasing substantiality (force/strength) and increasing subtlety (awareness). Progress in the ability to discharge progresses from the external to the evermore internal evidenced in the minimization of movement and the maximization of intention. The process that charcterizes the growth through these stages can be traced by what the object of consciousness is during each stage, where consciousness dwells, so to speak.

In the first stage, we learn to cultivate awareness of the internal structure of the human sphere as it functions in neutralizing and discharging physical energy (the *qi* level). We learn the dimension of the vertical circle of our sphere, the energy pathways and connections in the nine pearls and three springs of foundation, torso and sphere. We also learn the dimension of the horizontal circle of the human sphere, i.e. the energy pathways derived from the rotational aspect of the centerline.

In the second stage of development, awareness dwells in the center of the human sphere. Utilizing the sphere's integration to neutralize by unitary contraction into the center and discharging energy by unitary expansion from the center in the production of integral force.

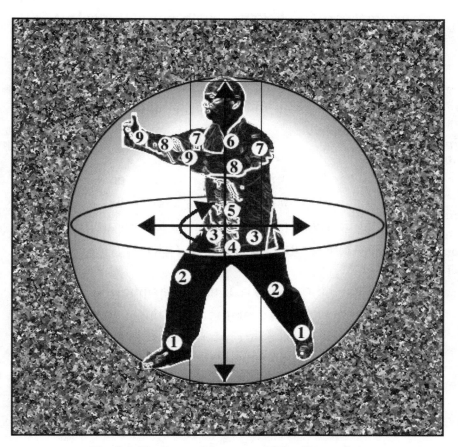

Fig. 9.4 The Internal Structure Of The Human Sphere

In the third stage, awareness dwells on the periphery of the human sphere. The quality of our touch is characterized more and more by lightness. This is the stage of "borrowing energy".

In the fourth stage, awareness dwells outside the periphery of our human sphere and is co-extensive with our energy field.

On the first level, the discharge of energy is on a purely external or *qi* level. Both strength and movement may be used. The first stage is purely external in that the discharge is accomplished in the physical integration of the three springs and the nine pearls, i.e. raising and closing of the centerline by closing the rear leg and straightening it while simultaneously filling the *mingmen*.

A first-level discharge starts in the feet and moves up through the ankle, knees, hips, lower back, middle back, upper back, shoulders, elbows, wrists, and is discharged from the hands into your opponent.

You can begin to get in touch with the energy flow by standing in *peng* or *an* position in archer step, and create a dynamic stillness in which all polarities are balanced and expanded internally to their limits. *(Fig. 9.4)*

First feel the energy axis from the opposing points on the periphery, from rear foot to palms. Then feel the opposing energy axis by pushing from the front foot back through the shoulder blades. Feel how they balance each other dynamically in stillness, the palms pushing as hard forward as the shoulder blades and *ming men* are pushing backwards, the front foot pushing as hard backward as the rear foot is pushing forward.

The knees are cooperating by opposing each other in opening and closing the structure, the *qi* is sinking along the lower part of the centerline into our foundation, anchoring it to the earth, and the spirit of awareness is rising along the upper part of the centerline to perceive our situation. All this occurs in the stillness of balanced polarities. Finally, feel how by tucking and sucking, the *mingmen* is expanded, producing integration and unitary expansion.

On the first level, what is felt in the hand is felt in the foot and what the foot does the hand does.

The flow of energy in discharging is exactly the reverse from neutralizing. The vertical half-circle of discharging "threads the pearls" from bottom to top. Discharging starts in the feet and moves up through the ankle, knees, hips, lower back, middle back, upper back, shoulders, elbows, wrists, and out the hands into your opponent.

In discharge, the neutralization sequence is reversed. First "close", then raise and shift the centerline forward by pushing from the rear leg into the front leg/foot, by straightening out, although not locking, the rear leg. This in effect allows A to get underneath B's push, uprooting him as A discharges his energy both upward and forward.

An important exception to the rule that the *yi* (intention) leads the *qi* (energy) is that when you start to discharge, from the first to the second pearl, from the ankle to the knee, the *qi* leads the *yi*. In other words, the physical action of the body in straightening the leg leads the *yi* because the physical movement triggers the mental component. Master Cai said that if in this part you try to use the intention to lead the energy, it will be too difficult to accomplish. Then, from the knee on up, the rule takes over and the *yi* leads the *qi*; the energy, movement, or form. When the energy reaches the lower spine, expand the *mingmen* to activate the torso spring and amplify the energy as it travels up the spine.

In discharging, when the energy reaches your neck, stretch the bowstrings of your body (the legs, the torso, and the arms) to the maximum, not physically, but intentionally. Once your bowstrings are extended all the way, you have many options such as throwing him away forward or pulling him down or to the side.

In the second level of skill in discharging, the intention originates in the *wuji* center where it is split immediately. Half goes down the legs to secure the root, and half goes up to be discharged at the point of contact with the opponent.

In deciding how to respond to a provocation, Master Cai said that "first use the minimum level of discharge by using integration through posture; if that is insufficient, you go to the second stage by adding spiral energy." What Master Cai means by the "discharge thru integration of posture" is the vertical dimension of the *peng* connection of hand to feet (or more generally, point of contact to root) mediated by the centerline. This is the first level. What is felt in the hand is felt in the foot and what the foot does the hand does. The force received by the sphere is grounded in the root and, rebounding from the earth, shoots back up and is discharged from the hands.

Spiral energy is created when the horizontal dimension (second level) of the *peng* connection ,constituted by the rotational aspect of the centerline, is added to the vertical. After all, a spiral is but the energetic union of the polar opposites of the linear and the circular. On an even more subtle and advanced level of working with *jin* (explosive strength), the spiral force is created by merely circling the knee to neutralize and discharge.

We cultivate strength slowly and deliberately. In its use in *fajin*, or attacking energy, the discharge is quick, a minifraction of a second, lasting no longer (upon sensing tension or instability in the opponent) than the time to have the intention . Hence the explosive nature of this use of *jin*.

The second level discharge is a simultaneous and omnidirectional expansion of the human structure which originates in the center and from there expands equally in all directions to the periphery.

Second Level: Sphericity & Unitary Expansion

The second level is where the awareness or consciousness component has begun to mix with and direct the physical. This is the level of *qi* and intention. In this second stage, movement is internalized and to stabilize the torso, attention is focused on the equal expansion of the torso to the front and the back when activating the *mingmen*. Visualize a wall against which your back is expanding, so that the push backwards is redirected forward while maintaining the centerline.

In the second level of skill in discharging, when you have achieved *peng* within the framework of the human cylinder, the intention originates in the *wuji* center where it is split immediately: half goes down the legs to secure the root at the point of contact with the earth, and half goes up to be discharged at the point of contact with the opponent.

In the second level, intention and stillness are added to the integration of the body's nine pearls and three springs. At this level, the discharge of the body's integral force is an expansion which originates in the *wuji* center of the organism and proceeds to the periphery. *(Fig. 9.5)* This is a unitary expansion, activated and controlled by filling or expanding the *mingmen*, which is of course the reason that Master Cai puts such high premium on developing awareness of the *mingmen* . Biomechanically, "filling the *mingmen* " activates the center joint of the body at the sacrolumbar junction and produces a voluntary muscular freezing or locking throughout the entire body.

To discharge, you should expand the parts that are opposite from the points of contact on your sphere.

The principle involved here is that to discharge, you always want to expand the parts that are opposite the points of contact on your sphere. This means that you must maintain the frame of the arms when being pushed upon, and fill the *mingmen* only in the lower back. Then the *jin* will actually discharge from the circle formed by the arms and hands.

Never think of discharging as expanding forward. Restrain your impulse to think forward, forward, forward. This will cause leaning and greediness. Instead, you must only think of expanding backwards, i.e. push out at the *mingmen* . Then the posture itself will conduct the impulse, and you will automatically expand forward in an equal amount and discharge at the periphery of the sphere/hands. For example, when Master Cai is doing *pengjin* or expanding energy in postures like single ward off and brush knee forward, he has a dual intention: one in the palm pressing down, and one in the *mingmen* with no intention in the hand/palm at the point of actual contact. The point of contact will accomplish the discharging automatically as the other two intentions expand

"The secret of using *yi* or intention is that both body and mind should be in a totally relaxed state to begin with, but at the moment of release the posture of the body should become firm, totally unmoveable, almost frozen."

Fig. 9.5 Unitary expansion of the sphere

the sphere while stabilizing its center.

According to Master Cai, one of the true secrets of the internal martial arts which distinguish them from the external martial arts lies in the qualitative difference between the initial impulse and the final discharge. In the internal martial arts, (i.e., when you know how to move from the center/line and use *yi*), the impulse to discharge, like a wave, starts weak in the center of the body and builds so that it is strongest just at the point of contact where it leaves the body. This is in sharp contrast to the external martial arts where the impulse is strongest at the beginning and then its force diminishes as it is discharged at the point of contact on the periphery.

Consider that the body's muscular system has a polarity structure. The dynamic tension of the body, which allows mobility, is created by a muscular structure that is paired and opposite. If you want to do a certain movement it requires the contraction of muscle (a) while its opposite member, muscle (b) is stretched and lenghtened. If you want to move back to the original position, than you must contract muscle (b), and muscle (a) will correspondingly be stretched and lenghtened.

To understand the anatomical and physiological mechanisms of discharging energy, keep in mind that discharge takes place in stillness, and not in movement. The question then becomes, if movement is produced by the simultaneous contracting-stretching actions of oppositely paired muscles, what muscle action, if any, is involved in the discharge of energy in stillness?

The answer lies in the fact that each individual muscle cell, and therefore the muscular system as an entity, has three options, not just two. Besides the ability to shorten in contraction and lengthen in stretching, each individual muscle cell has the ability to freeze or lock into place preventing either shortening or lengthening. In *Job's Body*,

204

Chapter 9 Using Stllness and Integration to Discharge Energy

Deane Juhan, writes that"..each individual muscle cell has only three options. It can shorten, it can lengthen, or it can lock into place preventing either motion…from these meager choices, muscle tissue produces all of the postures, gestures and qualitites of flesh of which we are capable. We stretch, we contract, and we lock into place; this is, in a nutshell, the entire gamut of our motor behavior."(p.116).

Master Cai described it in these words: "I'll tell you the secret of using *yi* or intention is that both body and mind should be in a totally relaxed state to begin with, but at the moment of release the posture of the body should become firm, totally unmovable, almost frozen." Regarding the first part of the statement, the necessity for being *song* or alertly relaxed, Master Cai added this clarification. "By relaxing all the muscles of the body, by relaxing the mind, relaxing both internally and externally, your *qi* will be able to flow according to your intention. Intention will lead or navigate the *qi*. The force I feel when I use intention is the *qi* being directed by my intention."

Next, the stillness that Master Cai talks about in discharge is not the stillness of the collapsed body. It is the stillness produced by the total simultaneous and instantaneous exertion of all the body's muscular cells locking themselves into place, freezing the body into a posture which literally becomes the embodiment of the mental intention that created it. Echoing the classics, Master Cai summarized, "at the moment of discharge, the *qi* (energy), the *jin* (strength) and the *yi* (intention) all come out at once, but the *yi* comes out first, because the *yi* (intention) leads the *qi* (energy)."

Being able to recognize the moment when you can discharge is very important. That moment is when your opponent goes from movement to stillness, when he stops moving. For instance, he stops moving, for however short a period of time, when he changes directions.

Third Level: Spherical Awareness & Peripheral Intentionality

The third level of awareness and development is that of pure intention without reference to *qi* or the use of strength. "In a practical sense," according to Master Cai, "to apply intention is a high development, the beginning of which is using one's integration and one's eyes." This, as we shall see, is the level of pure sphericity. Our awareness, certain of its center and its power, takes up a new dwelling place on the periphery of our sphere. *(Fig. 9.6)*

On the third level of skill, where you have a very good centerline and your foundation and sphere are developed properly, you don't have to worry about any of the numerous "rules" for proper posture and movement. Gradually, by practicing mindfulness, they become your "second nature", and then your "second nature" becomes your first or original nature. All movement will be completely natural, i.e. appropriate to the situation. When the awareness is properly trained, you don't have to worry about complicated "energy paths." Any point on the body can be *yin* and *yang* and able to neutralize and discharge. This is when you achieve true sphericity and become like

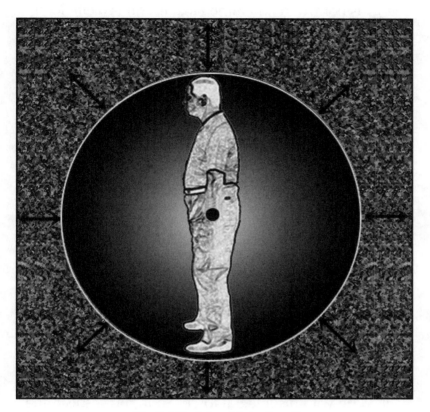

Fig. 9.6 Peripheral intentionality

a bouncing ball. By being in the moment when your opponent touches you, you "catch the time and bounce him away," as Master Cai would say.

Master Cai also explained this sphericity by saying that "the more circles I make internally, the more hands I have". His hand is going every which way internally while externally still. In this way "every point of your body is like a hand; you can discharge from it."

This is a level of accomplishment characterized by an extreme lightness of touch, because there is absolutely no exertion of strength. In a literal sense, the opponent's energy is borrowed and turned against him so efficiently that he pushes himself off your sphere. This lightness of touch and feeling naturally evolves into a state of no-touch feeling.

The term *kongjin (k'ung chin)* or empty force is used to describe two different phenomena. The first and lesser known refers to a method of disconnecting or emptying from an opponent. When you are playing pushhands with Master Cai, he will often break contact with you in such a way as to create a type of kinesthetic and perceptual vacuum into which one 's center is sucked uncontrollably and forcefully.

The result is an involuntary startle reflex, a loss of control and a feeling of total vulnerability in the face of Master Cai's superior awareness and physical ability, backed up with his integral force. So in this respect, the term "empty force" is descriptive in an ironic way. Since there is nothing there, nobody is touching any longer, it is obviously empty. The irony is that the energy or force that is moving us is our own, activated by Master Cai's awareness.

Briefly put, when his opponent is within striking distance, Master Cai is capable of controlling him without touching him. By neutralizing his opponent's intention with his awareness, and discharging his own intention, Master Cai is able to repel his opponent. The experience of this *kongin*, or empty force, is disconcerting in the extreme , and physically sickening to the stomach.

The explanation? When one's intention is neutralized by a superior awareness, we are rendered open and vulnerable to hostile penetrating forces. In fact, we are disabled by fear and the startle reflex takes over. We tense and consequently lose our awareness as well as our center, thereby leaving ourselves open to our opponent's mercy. Hence the frightening, sinking and nauseating feeling when experiencing the "empty force." You realize that your intention was being neutralized by his awareness as you were having it, or perhaps before you ever even had it!

In this way, the internal arts really operate in the psychological dimension. " It is because you don't initiate the attack that you can control everybody; and that control resides in your stillness, not your movement. Mentally you have to be calm when you are pushed. You must not think about it, just accept it and go with it, automatically relating it to your center and filling the back. It has to be reflexive, automatic, yet aware. At the place and time your opponent touches you, probe, find and go for the center instantaneously inducing resistance and frame and simultaneously discharging your integral force."

Fourth Level: Empty Force and

Interacting Fields of Awareness

From dwelling on the structure of our sphere in Level 1, our awareness moves to dwell in the center of our human sphere in Level 2, on the periphery of our sphere in Level 3. In the 4th and highest level of development, our awareness moves to dwell beyond the physical body into the outer fringes of our organismic field. On this level, the term *kongjin* or empty force refers to interaction at a distance in which one party seems to be manipulating the other at the end of an invisible rope.

In the Chinese tradition, this is the level where the *qi* and the *yi* or intention have been further refined into *shen* (spirit), which then expands to return and dwell in *wu* or nothingness. i.e. everywhereness. On the martial arts level, this is the level of *kongjin* (empty force), in which the master seems to be moving his opponents at will from a distance.

There are few practices in the Chinese martial arts that generate more dispute and controversy than the use of empty force. Some swear to its irresistability while others sneer at it as empty "farce". The truth is considerably more complex and subtle than these two extremes.

Investigation into the genesis and evolution of its practice show that *kongjin* is a perceptual game that develops field awareness. The practice of "empty force" will increase our awareness of ourselves and other people as nodes in interacting energy fields. This leads to consciously living everyday life in the truth that "nature is organized by evolving fields", to use Rupert Sheldrake's words. To practice is to utilize this knowledge, evolving a lifestyle, a way of being in the world, that makes our life more harmonious and growing in empathy and compassion.

Chapter 9 Using Stillness and Integration to Discharge Energy

Master Cai told me the story of how he first learned of "empty force" and later developed the ability. Mr. Le Huanzhi of Shanghai, the student of Tung Yingjie, one of Yang Chengfu's most prominent students, was famous for his empty force. Master Cai never personally witnessed Le Huanzhi doing it, but heard about his "empty force" ability through Le Huanzhi's son, who was Master Cai's college friend and fellow martial arts enthusiast and the author of one of the classic books on *taijiquan* entitled *The Essential Principle*,. Also one of Master Cai's own teachers, Mr. Guo Dadong (Kuo Ta Tung, Kuo Tai Tung), had been a student of Mr. Le Huanzhi (Leh Huan Chih, Lok Wan Ji) in the mid '50s and had personally experienced his "empty force."

Master Cai discovered how it worked for himself one day in 1974 in Guangdong. He was working with an exceptionally perceptive and sensitive student. It was almost by accident, Master Cai said, that once he used only his intention, exerting no physical force, and yet his student moved away! When he realized the implications of his discovery, he started a process of further experimentation and discovery. With some of his students and friends, he began a program of systematic practice in the training of awareness and intention.

Master Ha recalled his first experience with Master Cai's empty force while visiting him in Canton, China in 1979. "When I saw him working with his students, they would jump back 20-30 feet when he merely pointed at them. At first I could hardly believe my eyes, figuring it had to be either a miracle or a joke. But in discussing it with him, he explained to me that they were merely playing with the intention and its perception, in other words, with subtle energy, not irresistable force. Then when I played push-hands with his students, I quickly understood its value. They were so sensitive and quick that at that time I could not push them. They percieved and were able to neutralize my intention to push them the very moment I had it. That was a real eye opener."

The *taijiquan* system and tradition, particularly Yang style, is famous for its theoretical and practical emphasis on the neuro-sensory over the neuro-muscular. The traditional precept is that "awareness overcomes strength and technique." As manifested both in Le Huanzhi and Master Cai, development of empty force awareness is a logical outgrowth of this orientation of the *taijiquan* tradition. *Kongjin* or empty force is the logical and most refined extension or outgrowth of *tingjin (t'ing chin)*, or the abiltiy to listen to and interpret energy that we try to cultivate in pushhands practice.

When we begin pushhand practice, our touch is inevitably very heavy because we are still coming from the point of view of strength. But as we progress we begin to experience relaxation, and then softness overcomes strength and hardness. Pushhands becomes touchhands. As our touch naturally becomes lighter and lighter, we begin to understand how awareness overcomes technique. Taken to its extreme in *kongjin*, we no longer touch at all because the interplay occurs on the energetic level

212

between the two fields of awareness. The energy bubbles or spheres constituted by these fields of awareness are interacting beyond the level of their physical crystalizations.

In my own experience, because I had the opportunity to play a lot with Master Cai, I became extremely sensitized to the sphere of his physical influence, the space within his reach. Here, non-contact is more dangerous than contact, so that even when not touching, the field of our interacting awareneses is very charged, strong and powerful. I know that perceptually speaking, he has already disarmed me with his awareness, taking control of my center. In this relationship, he intends and I jump. Thus, empty force is the merger of and control over one field of awareness by another without physical contact.

The genesis of empty force is in the closely interpenetrating fields of a near contact situation. Its development results in distance field awareness. As familiarity increases, the range of play naturally extends out, at least in theory, infinitely stretching into the perceptual limits of our fields into more subtle interchange. Playing this game I would jump 20-30 feet by only a look from Master Cai.

In this game, the fields of the participants are interacting in a specific manner. There is a sender and a receiver. The rule of the game is the agreement between the sender and the receiver. Like a marionette on invisible strings, the receiver embodies, or acts out in movement, the perceived intent of the sender. If he perceives being pushed back, he goes back; if he perceives being pulled forward, he goes forward; if he perceives being shoved to the left or right, he will do so accordingly. If he perceives a somersault intention he will somersault; if he perceives a pirouette, he will pirouette. If he perceives a strong intention, he will react strongly; if he perceives a weak one, he will react in mild movement, etc.

The person moves only because he has agreed to do so under the rules of the game. What is really developed in this training is that very special type of awareness and sensitivity, the so-called sixth sense of field awareness which embraces but goes beyond its visual or auditory components.

This is dramatically illustrated in the kind of awareness that many blind people develop in compensation for the loss of sight. When you are in a room full of people that includes a blind person and you look at that blind person with a strong stare or intention, more likely than not that blind person will feel that somebody is looking at him/her and turn around or otherwise respond. Like many blind people, animals or so-called "primitive" people, also have retained this sixth sense of presence or awareness of intention.

When this game is observed by people who don't know what is going on, the tendency will be to focus on the sender and say, "Gee this guy is so powerful he can move people and make them do things from a distance." But in fact, everybody can be a sender while not everybody can be a receiver. So in this kind of practice, it is actually the receiving/perceiving skill that is being cultivated and practiced.

In the evolutionary scheme of things, the distance senses of vision and hearing developed after the proximity senses of touch and taste. In fact, vision can be thought of as an extension of the sense of touch, a form of touching at a distance. Its survival value, obviously, consists of giving us quicker information regarding possible threats to our being before the threat is literally upon us, giving us more time to prepare and activate our defense systems.

In the Chinese tradition, *shen*, meaning "spirit", is considered the ultimate and most subtle refinement of *qi*, or life energy. Mirroring the Western saying that "the eyes are the mirror of the soul," the Chinese also believe that both our *shen* (spirit) and our *yi* (will or intention) are manifested in and through our eyes. The eyes and their use, therefore, merit very special consideration in any discussion of *taijiquan* pushhand and field play training and their implications for the conduct of our being in the world.

In a martial arts situation, whether in pushhand training or in actual combat, Master Cai warns not to lock eyes with your opponent. "To use the eyes directly that way is to react and set up resistance and conflict. Your gaze should be directed inward, not outward; it should be receptive and not projective."

When confronting an opponent, by keeping a soft focus anywhere else, say on his chest or belly, you can use your peripheral vision to feel or sense the totality of his being and take his energy down into your center, thus neutralizing him with your vision, with your *shen*, or spirit, even before touching him. In field awareness play, this relationship by mututal agreement is extended to the fringes of our fields of visual and nonvisual awareness.

Master Cai's views on this subject are a logical extension of the *taiji* philosophy as pertaining to both our conduct of daily life and martial art situations. He counsels the cultivation of soft, or *yin* eyes, as opposed to hard or *yang* eyes. "In all of the activities of daily life", he says, "your eyes must be receptive and simply take the world in; they must not be habitually in an intense focus of concentration".

The only time when the eyes should become hard and focused is during the very brief moment of discharge, whether it is the discharge of integral physical force in contact, or the discharge of pure intention at a distance in field awarenesss. In the first case, your eyes project your intention outward into or through and beyond your opponent, leading the concentrated *qi*, or *jin*, to explode at its target. However, immediately after the discharge, the eyes relax and become soft again. In the second case, the intention was merely sent and received over a distance primarily by the eyes.

This also helps to clarify the true benefits of *kongjin* play. Anybody can look across the room with a strong intention. But the ability to feel that intention as an intrusion into the field of awareness is possessed by very few indeed. It has been civilized out of us.In empty force field awareness play, we develop the ability to sense fields because obviously this ability has great usefulness in the martial arts.

Appendix I: List of Chinese Names and Words

NAMES

Pinyin	**Wade-Giles**	**Other**
蔡松芳 Cai Songfang	Ts'ai Sung Fang	Choy Soong Fong
陳微明 Chen Weiming	Ch'en Wei Ming	Chan Mei Ming
董英傑 Dong Yingjie	Tung Ying Chieh	
方乃立 Fang Naili		
郭火棟 Guo Dadong	Kuo Ta Tung	Kuo Tai Tung
韓星垣 Han Xingyuan	Han Hsing Yuan	
乐幻智 Le Huanzhi	Leh Huan Chih	Lok Wan Ji
王香斋 Wang Xiangzhai	Wang Hsiang Chai	
夏長苓 Fong Ha	Xia Changfang	Hsia Ch'ang Fang

Pinyin	Wade-Giles	Other
楊澄甫 Yang Chengfu	Yang Ch'eng Fu	
楊健侯 Yang Jianhou	Yang Chien Hou	
楊俊敏 Yang Jingming	Yang Ching Ming	Yang Jwing-Ming
楊祿禪 Yang Luchan	Yang Lu Ch'an	
楊守中 Yang Shouzhong	Yang Shou Chong	Yeung Sau Choong
楊振鐸 Yang Zhenduo	Yang Chen Tuo	
葉大密 Ye Dami	Yeh Ta Mi	Yip Da Me
尤彭熙 Yu Pengxi	Yu P'eng Hsi	
張三丰 Zhang Sanfeng	Chang San Feng	
鄭曼青 Zheng Manqing	Cheng Man Ch'ing	

WORDS

Pinyin	Wade-Giles	Other
按 an	an	
八卦 bagua	pa kua	
八卦掌 baguazhang	pa kua chang	
採 cai	ts'ai	
纏絲勁 chansijin	ch'an ssu chin	
抽絲勁 chousijin	ch'ou ssu chin	
丹田 dantian	tan t'ien	
督脈 dumai	tu mai	tou mei
發勁 fajin	fa chin	
功夫 gongfu	kung fu	
涵胸拔背 hankong babei	han kung pa pei	

Pinyin	Wade-Giles	Other
会阴 huiyin	hui yin	
挤 ji	chi	
劲 jin	chin	jing
精 jing	ching	
靠 kao	k'ao	
空劲 kongjin	k'ung chin	
胯 kua	k'ua	
揽雀尾 lanquewei	lan ch'ueh wei	
劳宫 laogong	lao kung	
力 li	li	
捌 lie	lieh	

Pinyin	Wade-Giles	Other
擴 lu	lu	
命门 mingmen	ming men	
內家拳 neijiaquan	nei chia ch'uan	
逆纏丝勁 ni chansijin	ni ch'an ssu chin	
掤 peng	p'eng	
掤勁 pengjin	p'eng chin	
崩拳 pengquan	p'eng ch'uan	
氣 qi	ch'i	
氣功 qigong	ch'i kung	
氣海 qihai	ch'i hai	
拳 quan	ch'uan	

Pinyin	Wade-Giles	Other
任脉 renmai	jen mai	
yin mei		
神 shen	shen	
師傅 shifu	shih fu	sifu
試力 shili	shih li	
十三势 shisan shi	shih san shih	
順纏絲勁 shun chansijin	shun ch'an ssu chin	
鬆 song	sung	
太極 taiji	t'ai chi	tai chi
太極拳 taijiquan	t'ai chi ch'aun	
推手 tuishou	t'ui shou	

Pinyin	Wade-Giles	Other
無 wu	wu	
無極 wuji	wu chi	
形意 xingyi	hsing i	
形意拳 xingyiquan	hsing yi ch'uan	
意 yi	i	
易経 yijing	I Ching	
易筋経 yijinjing	i chin ching	
陰陽 yin-yang	yin-yang	
意拳 yiquan	i ch'uan	
詠春 yongchun	yung ch'un	

Pinyin	Wade-Giles	Other
肘 zhai	chai	
站橋 zhanzhuang	chan chuang	
三点 zhongding	chung ting	
肘 zhou	chou	

Order Form

Please send _____ *additional copies of WARRIORS OF STILLNESS, VOL.1, to:*

Name: _____

Address : _____

City: _____

State: _____ *Zip:* _____

Please make checks payable and send to:
Center For Healing & The Arts
2329 Boulevard Circle
Walnut Creek, CA 94595

I enclose a check for the total of: $ _____

This was calculated as follows:

                             (No.of books) _____ *x $24.95=$* _____

Shipping & handling:

☐   *U.S. $3.50 first book, each additional book $2.00=$* _____

☐ *foreign orders:$10.00 first book; each additional book $5.00 =$* _____

                  Cal . sales tax (if applicable)@ 7.25%=$ _____

                                       total: $ _____